# Una Sancta

# Una Sancta

## Why Are We Still Separated?

CORMAC BRIAN O'DUFFY

*Forewords by*
*Anders Cardinal Arborelius OCD*
*and Karin Johannesson*
*and Elisabeth Peeters*

RESOURCE *Publications* · Eugene, Oregon

UNA SANCTA
Why Are We Still Separated?

Copyright © 2025 Cormac Brian O'Duffy. All rights reserved. Except for brief quotations in critical publications or reviews, no part of this book may be reproduced in any manner without prior written permission from the publisher. Write: Permissions, Wipf and Stock Publishers, 199 W. 8th Ave., Suite 3, Eugene, OR 97401.

Resource Publications
An Imprint of Wipf and Stock Publishers
199 W. 8th Ave., Suite 3
Eugene, OR 97401

www.wipfandstock.com

PAPERBACK ISBN: 979-8-3852-4045-6
HARDCOVER ISBN: 979-8-3852-4046-3
EBOOK ISBN: 979-8-3852-4047-0

VERSION NUMBER 03/20/25

# PERMISSIONS

I am grateful to Sister Annemarie Bäumler and the Christköniginstitut in Meitingen for all materials relating to the work of Catholic priest and Martyr, Blessed Max Josef Metzger (1877–1944) I am especially grateful for the use of the talk "Why are we still separated?" given by Metzger in Dresden in 1941 which originally inspired this book. My wife and I are grateful for all their love and continuous support in this venture.

Permission to use excerpts of *The Role of the Augsburg Confession Catholic and Lutheran Views* Edited by Joseph A. Burgess given by Fortress Press of Philadelphia

Permission to use excerpts of the *Ecumenical Vanguard* by Prof Leonard Swidler and *The Priest and the Führer* by Leonard Swidler and Cormac O'Duffy given by ILP Publishers.

Efforts were made regarding excerpts from the book of Rev. Max Lackmann *The Augsburg Confession and Catholic Unity* 1959/1963 with publishers Herder and Herder. This did not produce any copyright information as the book is long out of print. On advice from Herder extensive efforts have been made to contact members of the family of Max Lackmann but as yet have not produced any results.

All quotations from the Augsburg Confession, the Apology published by Concordia are in public domain. *The Augsburg Confession A Collection of Sources* by Johann Michael Reu 1930 published by Concordia is in public domain. The collection includes both Johann Eck's 404 Theses and The Confutation.

Thanks due to my good friend, Monsignor Lubomir Žák of the Max Josef Metzger Center in Olomouc in the Czech Republic for the German text of the *Muß die Glaubensspaltung Sein?* "Why are we separated?' talk mentioned above.

# Warum noch Glaubensspaltung?

Darüber spricht am Sonntag, den 16. Novbr., nachm. 5 Uhr

## Dr. Max Josef Metzger

von der Bruderschaft Una Sancta in der Kath. Hofkirche

**Alle gläubigen Christen sind dazu herzlich eingeladen!**

<small>Verantwortlich für den Inhalt: Wilhelm Beier, Dresden — Druck: Germania Buchdruckerei, Dresden</small>

A poster of a talk to be given by Blessed Max Josef Metzger in Dresden's Catholic Cathedral on Sunday November 16th, 1941. This was two years before his arrest and final execution in 1944 for his stand for Peace and Christian Unity. The German title literally means "Why are we [Christians] still separated?" At that time in 1941, the SS had appropriated over 300 monasteries and institutions, clergy were being watched, arrested and sent to concentration camps and Catholic schools, press, trade unions, political parties and youth leagues were being eliminated.

Dedicated to the memory of all those Catholics, Lutherans and others who have sought to heal the schism in Western Christianity since the failure of the Diet of Augsburg in 1530. In particular this Book is dedicated to the memory of two pioneers who have sought a path back to Christian Unity: Lutheran Pastor Rev Max Lackmann (1910–2000) and Blessed Max Josef Metzger (1887–1944.)

> Catholic brothers in faith, become evangelical! Not that you should leave the Catholic Church, but that you should fulfill its real and ultimate calling. Evangelical renewal, a thorough Christianization of the Church is the essential prerequisite, so that the serious Christian of the Evangelical Church may recognize that here is Christ and his Gospel pure and unfalsified, in full unbroken vital power. Evangelical brothers, become Catholic! Free yourselves from negative protestation, from pre-judgement, from all narrowness of national and racist attachment! . . . Catholics become evangelical! Evangelicals become Catholic! Then there will be the *Una Sancta*, the one holy Church for which we jointly strive and pray."[1]
>
> Blessed Max Josef Metzger (1887–1944)

We say Yes to tradition and no to traditionalism, Yes to the office of the Pope, and no to papalism. Yes, to the canon of the Church, no to legalism. To Mary the most blessed Mother of God we say Yes! But we must say no to Marianism! Yes, to the institution of the Church and to episcopacy, confession etc., but no to institutionalism. Yes, to the abundant grace of the holy sacraments and to the sacramental character of the Church: no to sacramentalism. Yes, to Rome as the central See, but no to centralism and Romanism.[2]

Rev Max Lackmann (1910–2000)

---

1. Swidler, *Blood witness*, 71.
2. Asmussen, *Unfinished*, 106.

Allow us to express our affection for you and to call you our sons and brothers . . . We address you, then, as brothers even though you are separated from us. For as St Augustine said: "Whether they like it or not, they are our brothers. They will only cease to be our brothers when they cease to say: Our Father.[3]

Pope Saint John XXIII (1881–1963)

It could never be that so large a portion of Christendom should have split off from the communion of Rome and kept up a protest for three hundred years for nothing. . .All aberrations are founded on and have their life in some truth or other, and Protestantism, so widely spread, so long enduring, must have in it, and must be a witness of a great truth or much truth."[4]

Cardinal Saint John Henry Newman (1801–1890)

---

3. Pope Saint John XXIII *Ad Petri Cathedram*, 86.
4. Newman, *Apologia*, 188.

# Contents

List of Photo Illustrations | xi
Foreword by Anders Cardinal Arborelius OCD
 and Karin Johannesson | xiii
Foreword by Elisabeth Peeters | xvii
Preface: Why Are We Still Separated? | xix
Acknowledgements | xxiii
Introduction | xxv

1  The Conversion of Luther | 1
2  The Relevance of the Augsburg Confession Today | 9
3  The Historical Records of the Augsburg Confession | 17
4  The Diet of Augsburg 1530 | 27
5  The Confutation | 35
6  Fateful Days | 41
7  The Confession Spreads | 50
8  Attempts at Reconciliation | 57
9  The Healing of the Divide | 72
10 Max Lackmann: Author of 'The Augsburg
   Confession and Catholic Unity" | 80
11 Blessed Max Joseph Metzger (1887–1944) and
   the Una Sancta Movement | 96
12 The Tide Begins to Turn | 108
13 The Academic Path to Unity after Vatican 2 | 121

CONTENTS

14   Breakthrough! 1999–2030?  |  139

*Afterword: A Reflection by Blessed Max Josef Metzger, Martyr for
        Christian Unity, Dresden Hofkirche November 1941*  |  147
*About the Author*  |  155
*Bibliography*  |  157

## List of Photo Illustrations

1. Poster of meeting of Blessed Max Metzger in Dresden Catholic Cathedral on Sunday November 16th, 1941, *Warum Noch Glaubensspaltung?* (Why are we still divided?) courtesy of Sister Anne Marie Baumlier of the Christkoenig Institute in Meitingen. Germany. | vi

2. Photo of Fr Max Metzger (1887–1944) 50th birthday. Courtesy Sister Anne Marie, Christkönig Institute, Meitingen Germany. | xxiv

3. Luther House in Wittenburg, photo from Creative Commons. | 2

4. Priests in Dachau. Photo No 83818, from the United States Holocaust Memorial Museum. Permission being sought for use. | 7

5. Augsburg Confession cover by Christan Beyer. German Wikipedia, Augsburger Reichstag. Public Domain. | 27

6. Augsburg Confession. Woodcut created in Wittenberg 1530 Courtesy Dominic Winters Gloucester, U.K. | 34

7. Phillip Melanchthon (1487–1560) Artist: Lucas Cranach the Elder 1532 Gemäldegalerie Alte Meister, Kassel. Public Domain | 47

8. Peace of Augsburg Front page of Document, Mainz 1555. Print of Augsburg Imperial and Religious peace 'Say goodbye to the Romans' Wikimedia Commons. | 53

9. Europe in 1560 Historical Atlas: William R. Shepherd, 1926. Public Domain. | 56

10. Martin Chemnitz: Portrait by Ludger Tom Ring the Younger 1569. Wikimedia Commons. | 63

## List of Photo Illustrations

11. Diogo de Pavia de Andrade: Medal from the Church of the Convent of Grace, burial place of Diogo. Wikipedia | 64

12. Book of Fr John Dez SJ seeking reconciliation between Lutherans and Catholics in Strasbourg 1688. Permission sought from Mainz Gutenberg Library. | 72

13. Rev. Max Lackmann (1910–2000). From cover of Book 'The Augsburg Confession and Catholic Unity' Herder and Herder. Unable to source owner of photo. | 81

14. Max Lackmann's Prison Record in Dachau Concentration Camp. File: Max Lackmann Dachau Arolsen Archives DocID90419613.jpg. Creative Commons Attribution-Share Alike 4.0 International | 87

15. Blessed Max Josef Metzger (1887–1944) as German Army Chaplain. Courtesy of Sister Annemarie Bäumler, Meitingen, Germany. | 97

16. The Frauenkirche in Dresden before and after restoration. Public Domain Photos. | 120

17. Cardinal Koch (DPCU) and Rev. Anne Burghardt in Poland 19 September 2023. Photo LWF Albin Hillert with permission. | 144

18. The Sack of Magdeburg 1631: Die Magdeburger Hochzeit. Painting from workshop of Matthäus Merian (1593–1650) Imperial (Catholic) troops under Tilly conquer the redoubt and suburbs of Magdeburg. Public Domain. | 148

19. Ecumenical gathering in Lund Sweden in 2017 to commemorate the 500th anniversary of the posting of Martin Luther's 95 Theses in October 2017. Including Dr Martin Junge LWF General Secretary, with Bishop Munib Younan, President of LWF, Pope Francis, Bishop Anders Arborelius and Cardinal Kurt Koch. (Paul Haring CNS Permission sought) | 150

20. The Grieving Magdeburg Dir Traurende Magdeburg in the entrance of Johannes Kirche Magdeburg. Creative Commons Attribution-Share Alike 4.0 International Olaf Meister. | 154

21. Cormac O'Duffy—author—in the Dresden Hofkirche where Metzger gave his talk on Christian Unity. Photo Dieter and Alice Rettschlag, Wachau, Saxony, Germany. | 155

# Foreword

Twenty-five years ago, Catholics and Lutherans came to an important agreement in Augsburg: we really share the same faith; Christ justifies us through his grace. For most Christians today, this is something obvious, but during and after the Reformation it was a very difficult issue. Lutherans thought that Catholics paid too much attention to human merits and Catholics thought that Lutherans did not pay enough attention to our human answer to God's grace. Of course, this is a simplification of a very complicated dispute, but in Augsburg, this fight came to an end, even if there can be some minor different accents in Lutheran and Catholic theology. We must be very grateful that one of the main difficulties regarding our common understanding of faith has come to an end. This fact gives us the possibility to speak with one voice when we proclaim the good message that Jesus Christ is our Redeemer, who has come to justify us through the gift of faith. Thanks to this grace, we can grow in holiness and become more and more transformed in Christ. All the baptized are called to be sanctified. This common understanding is especially important for our Christian anthropology and spirituality. Today we see that Christians of different denominations are very united when it comes to prayer and spiritual life. Holiness goes together with unity. The more we are united to Christ the more we will also be united with other Christians. A Saint like Thérèse of Lisieux formulates this in one of her poems, something that can be accepted by most Lutherans. A Lutheran nun even described her as the 'Catholic answer to Luther': "I need a heart burning with tenderness, who will be my support forever, who loves everything in me, even my weakness. . . And who never leaves me day and night. . . I must have a God who takes on my nature and becomes my brother and is able to suffer! . . . Ah! I know well, all our righteousness is worthless in yoursight... So, I, for my purgatory, choose your burning love, O heart of my God! (Poem 23)

Thérèse was declared Doctor of the Church, which means that she has a message of universal importance for all Christians. Even if she might be looked upon more as having a message for our spiritual life, this fact implies that she has also something to say on the dogmatical level. Similarly, a dogmatic document such as the Augsburg Confession can inspire and challenge us in our spiritual life. The Augsburg Confession (Confessio-Augustana) is the most prominent and influential of the Lutheran confessional writings. It was mainly written by Philip Melanchthon (1497–1560) and was presented to Emperor Charles V at the Diet of Augsburg in 1530. It aims toshow that Lutheran theology is not sectarian or schismatic but based on the Bible and consistent with the tradition of the Church. In our spiritual life, the concluding words of the seventh article of the Augsburg Confession can be a fruitful subject for meditation. In this article it is made clear that it is not necessary "for true unity of the Christian church that ceremonies instituted by men be uniformly observed everywhere, as Paul says to the Ephesians in Chapter 4: "One body, one Spirit, as you were called to one and the same hope of your call, one Lord, one faith, one baptism." Today, Lutherans and Catholics agree on the importance and interpretation of the doctrine of justification, which is the most decisive dogmatical article according to Martin Luther. This consensus invites us to explore, in our spiritual life, what this might mean for the unity and common mission of the Church as the 500th anniversary of the publication of the Augsburg Confession approaches.The ecumenical impact and message of our shared understanding of God's salvific, justifying, and sanctifying action is very important. Today Christians of different backgrounds can give the same hopeful message to our secular world. Hopefully, this can also imply that we can work together on the level of evangelization. Of course, this can be more difficult and demanding. Still, itwould be a real prophetical sign for our contemporary society, where polarization and extreme ideologies are so widely spread. This poor world of ours needs Jesus Christ and his gospel more than ever. One of the big difficulties for people of today to be open to Christian faith is that we Christians do not appear as united, but as widely different and incompatible. Spiritual ecumenism can inspire us to find a way of evangelizing together. This should be the natural consequence of our common understanding of the doctrine of justification.There are also signs of this common proclamation of the Christian message tothe world

## Foreword

of today. On November 17, 2024, the German Catholic priest Max Joseph Metzger was beatified as martyr in Freiburg in Breisgau. He was beheaded by the Nazis in Brandenburg in 1944. He had promoted the ecumenical movement *Una Sancta* and worked for peace together with many Protestants. He can help us to see how we as Christians of different denominations can bring us to give a common witness to our faith, through our shared understanding of the mystery of justification and sanctification—even in a society where Christian values are denied or unknown. His example can inspire us today to see more clearly that our spiritual life in a secular society helps us to become authentic witnesses of Jesus. The intimate process of Justification and sanctification must become outwardly visible and evident in a concrete life of justice and peace, in faith, hope, and charity.

This book, written by Cormac O'Duffy, can be very helpful for all Christians of today, so that they can be imbued by this mystery of justification and its consequences. If we grow closer to Jesus and become more and more transformed by his grace, we can become authentic messengers and prophetic signs in our world of today. O'Duffy wants to show Christians of all denominations and traditions that we have more in common than many of us may realize. If we allow the Holy Spirit to inspire us to follow Jesus more faithfully and be justified and sanctified by his grace, we can transmit something of his love and mercy to the secular society of today.

**Anders Cardinal Arborelius**
Bishop in the Catholic Diocese of Stockholm

**Karin Johannesson**
Bishop in the Evangelical-Lutheran diocese of Uppsala

# Foreword

THIS IS A BOOK that stands out in many ways. It is one of few books I would like to see in the hands of as many Christians as possible: church leaders and ministers of every denomination, and indeed every Christian who deeply cares about overcoming the rifts and divisions of the past that continue to separate us despite the huge progress that has been made.

Today, once more, our world appears to be falling apart, driven by the power hunger and disdain for truth, humaneness, and compassion of a few strongmen, exposing the weakness and defenselessness of a social order that either has managed to evict God, or confounds the Christian faith with narrow-minded nationalism. This world bitterly needs our common Christian witness of a unity that is both visible and willing to embrace our diversity as a creative and mutually enriching gift of the Holy Spirit to us all.

This book goes a long way towards enabling us to grow in this spirit. It is not just a passionate plea for a visible sign of unity and reconciliation to mark the 500thanniversary of the *Confessio Augustana* on June 25th, 2030. It also helps pave the way.

The brilliant and well-balanced analysis of the tragic events that led up to the schism in Augsburg in 1530 is the first eye-opener. As the author takes the reader along on a profoundly moving and very well-documented journey through history, it is impossible not to become aware of the full scope of a tragedy never intended by the Lutheran reform movement that understood itself as a much-needed spiritual renewal *within* the Church. Likewise the reader discovers how much common ground has already been reached. Today the CA no longer stands between us as the big obstacle it was assumed to be, but in actual fact never was.

# Foreword

After highlighting the ground-breaking work started as early as the C17th by Jean Dez and taken up again in the C20th by the spearheads of the Ecumenical Movement on both sides of the divide, the author humbly formulates his hope as a rhetorical question: *"Catholic- Lutheran unity didn't happen in 1980. . . However, after the Joint Declaration of Justification of 1999, could we be hopeful that it might happen in 2030—the 500th anniversary of the Augsburg Confession?"*

Cormac O'Duffy is not just extremely well informed; he is also a realist. He is well aware of the fact that this would not yet be the final goal. However, it would be huge step towards reaching true reconciliation and visible unity among all Christians. Ultimately, to quote from the "Afterword" citing Blessed Max Joseph Metzger's sermon in Dresden Hofkirche in November, 1941: *"Only from the grace of God can we expect and ask for what is 'impossible to man'"*.

There are no words to express my admiration and gratefulness for the immense effort that must have gone into this volume. It is the best contribution I have seen to an issue so dear to God's heart, and at the same time it is the most well-written and accessible one. May it reach as many readers as possible and fire them up with a Spirit of reconciliation, mutual understanding, and a passionate desire for visible unity in diversity!

**Elisabeth Peeters**, Discalced Carmelite
Kirchzarten, Germany February 28, 2025

# Preface
## Why Are We Still Separated?

AT AN ECUMENICAL SERVICE with the Pontifical Council for Christian Unity and the Lutheran World Federation held in Poland in 2023, the General Secretary of the Federation formally called for a joint reflection by both Churches on the Augsburg Confession—*Confessio Augustana* or CA—, the basic doctrinal statement of the Lutheran faith. Though this document was first reviewed by Catholic and Lutheran theologians at the time of the Diet of Augsburg in 1530 and rejected, there has not been any official joint study by both churches from that time to the present. Cardinal Kurt Koch, Prefect of the Vatican Dicastery for Promoting Christian Unity, and Rev. Anne Burghardt, the General Secretary of the Federation, therefore suggested such "a common reflection could lead to another milestone on the way from conflict to communion."[1] They were reflecting a hope expressed by Pope Francis that a joint study of the Augsburg Confession in preparation for the document's 500th anniversary in 2030 could strengthen Catholic and Lutheran ability to confess together what joins them in faith. He said, "it will be important to examine with spiritual and theological humility the circumstances that led to the divisions, trusting that, although it is impossible to undo the sad events of the past, it is possible to reinterpret them as a part of a reconciled history."[2] In saying this, Pope Francis was carrying on the tradition of his predecessor Pope Saint John Paul II, who acknowledged

---

1. Common Word Preparing for 500th Anniversary of Augsburg Confession. https://lwfassembly.org

2. Vatican News June 25 2021 Pope Francis with Archbishop Panti Filibus Musa President of the Lutheran World Federation. In https://www.vaticannews.va/en/pope/news/2021–26/pope-francis-world-lutheran-federation-conflict-to-communion.html Accessed 10/29/24

the faults of the church in history and asked the faithful not to hold biased views of history. This Pope Francis held would prevent genuine reconciliation between the sides affected by past divisions.

The following recounting of the story of the Augsburg Confession is written to help the lay person to understand the background and history of the CA, and to appreciate its need for joint review and possible agreement before its 500th anniversary in 2030. It does not seek to answer the questions that will be discussed by either the Augustana Working Group of the International Lutheran Council or the Work Group of the Lutheran World Federation with the Dicastery for Promoting Christian Unity that have been established for this historic purpose. The story of the circumstances of the Diet of Augsburg are hardly known by modern Catholics and Lutherans and it could easily be said that they would hardly affect the church going habits of either confession. One could not imagine any person today deciding on church affiliation purely on the basis adherence ( or non-adherence) to the Augsburg Confession. However, the sad thing is that the failure to agree together at Augsburg in 1530 had enormous consequences in both the history of Europe (and thus the world) and in the wider Church. As a result of the peace of Augsburg in 1555, Germany was divided into a patchwork of Catholic and Lutheran states. According to Lee Wandell, in the year 1500, any Christian could travel from one end of Europe to another without any difficulty or fear of persecution. By 1600 this was no longer possible as every form of Christianity was now illegal somewhere in Europe.[3] It also did not take more than 100 years for the Protestant and Catholic States in Europe to go to war with each other, creating between 6 and 16 million deaths in the French Wars of religion (1562–1598) and in the German Thirty Years war (1618–1648). Confessionally the once unified Church was now severed into many pieces, with each part continuing the process of division into new and different churches.[4] Denominationalism

---

3. Wandell, Lee Palmer (2011) *The Reformation* Cambridge University Press *apud* Leithart, Peter (18 April 2017). "How the Reformation Failed". *Theopolis Institute*. Quoted in https://en.wikipedia.org/wiki/Reformation. It is interesting to note in this regard the Schengen agreement which now allows such uninhibited travel across Europe in the European Union. The idea of the European Union itself—whatever its secular nature—was inspired by Catholic and Protestant politicians. https://international.la-croix.com/news/politics/europes-founding-fathers-were-inspired/9968

4. Wesleyan University estimates there are over 33,000 different denominational groups in global Christianity ranging from one billion (Catholics) to several churches as little as 100 members each. https://www.wesleyan.edu/christianitystudies/pathways/world.html

was born, which went against the heart of Jesus words in his final priestly prayer in John 17—that "they might be one so that the world might believe".

We live in a blessed time: many are seeking to repair all these divisions, both politically (for example in the creation of the European Union) and in the Churches, through various ecumenical movements and groups. As Cardinal Koch and Rev. Burghardt suggested, resolving the question of the Augsburg Confession could be another milestone on the path 'from conflict to communion.'

The following historical account is not an easy read: there were many things said on both sides of the schism which were regrettable, and not ostensibly spoken in a spirit of love, thus leading to division, acrimony, name calling and indeed war and destruction. It is, however, the conviction of the author that the facts in history must be faced to enable true reconciliation. Therefore, we wait in hope with the Lutheran World Federation, The International Lutheran Council and the Dicastery for Promoting Christian Unity, that by the 500th anniversary of the Augsburg Confession, substantial agreement may be reached on its articles, and that the 25th of June 2030 will be marked with a joyful celebration of imperfect (as yet) union of the Church.

# Acknowledgements

I AM INDEBTED TO all the many writers and thinkers who have been dealing with the question of the Augsburg Confession for many years. Many have sought Catholic-Lutheran reconciliation from the time of the Diet of Augsburg until recently. There are many Catholic priests and writers, such as Father Jean Dez in the 17th century, Father Josef Lortz and Karl Adam in the 20th century, Lutherans Hans Asmussen and the authors of the *Sammlung* collection, Max Lackmann, Ernst Fincke, Richard Baumann, and Wolfgang Lehmann. More recently there are new authors and leaders such as Archbishop Jaeger, Cardinal Bea, Vinzenz Pfnür, Wolfhart Pannenberg, and my friend Leonard Swidler, who invited me to help reissue his book on Metzger. Also of note are Cardinal Walter Kasper, and Harry McSorley, and the works of all the recent popes from Paul VI to Pope Francis. I am indebted to Professors Robert Kolb and Joel Elowsky of Concordia Lutheran Seminary in St. Louis for their help in researching this book. Thanks too to Fr Joe Tedesco of Mepkin Trappist Abbey SC and Msgr. Edward Lofton who encouraged my research and music dedicated to Metzger. Thanks to Whitney Lewis and the staff at Dorchester Public Library in Summerville who have helped me find so many sources I needed for my text. I am grateful too to Bishop Karin Johannesson and Cardinal Arborelius from Sweden who so kindly wrote the Foreword. I must always thank my wife Fiona for all her wisdom and sound advice in my writing and in helping painstakingly to prepare the final text. Grateful thanks also to my friend Ray Sheldrake of Christchurch New Zealand for preparing the photos for the text.

Two authors who, in my opinion, are the most important in this entire reconciliation process are the Lutheran pastor Max Lackmann of the

## Acknowledgements

*Sammlung* and priest and martyr Blessed Max Josef Metzger. I dedicate this book especially to their memory.

Finally we offer our love and thanks to Sister Annemarie and the Community of Christköniginstitut Meitingen and the late Sister Gertraud Roßmann, Archivist of the Community, who helped to start us on this path of discovery.

# Introduction

IN EARLY NOVEMBER 1941 German peace activist and priest Dr. Max Josef Metzger made his way from his home in the Christ Koenig Community to Dresden, the Capital of Saxony. There he was scheduled to give an address to the assembled Dresden Christian gathering at the Catholic Hofkirche. The title given to the talk was in German "Warum noch Glaubensspaltung?"—meaning 'Why is there still a division of faith?"—or perhaps more simply: "Why is there still no Christian unity?" It was a provocative title, and it was meant to provoke. While Metzger was a trained intellectual with a Doctorate in Theology, he was more an activist for Christian causes. One of his greatest causes was indeed the quest for Christian unity. He saw Christian disunity as a tragedy, and while others had written and analyzed it from different perspectives trying to understand its root causes, Metzger wanted to do something about it. In the situation of Nazi Germany he had realized that a divided Church was too weak to confront the menace of Naziism and the reign of terror, and so he set out himself to try to repair the broken Church and to bring it back to a sense of unity. He had no special commissioning for such work from any Bishop or from the German hierarchy; no laying on of hands or specially delegated pastoral duty.[1] He just looked for his support from his Lord and Savior and started to follow his call.

---

1. His Archbishop in Freiburg Conrad Gröber, was an early known supporter of the Nazi regime and was nicknamed the 'Brown Bishop'. He said that, while he once viewed Metzger as an 'idealist', he now 'lamented his offence' of crimes against the Nazi regime. According to Wikipedia, Gröber did make some other unsuccessful efforts to mitigate the death penalty. Wikipedia article. https://en.wikipedia.org/wiki/Conrad_Grober.

# Introduction

Blessed Max Josef Metzger 1887–1944

Over the years 1941–43, he gave talks and worked with groups all over Germany, forming an ecumenical *Una Sancta Brotherhood* as a result.[2] This group was neither Catholic nor Lutheran nor confessional, but, rather, a fellowship of Christian believers from all Christian backgrounds, lay and ordained, working together to bring the churches together. He had learnt from his first such group held in his hometown of Meitingen just how close believers in Christ may be, irrespective of denominational backgrounds, when gathered in unity, fellowship, praise and prayer.

The world in which he was raised in Schopfheim in Baden Württemberg, was very different. German states followed the religious affiliation of their rulers, and Catholics were a small minority in this largely Protestant town. They had no Catholic parish from 1557 to 1846, following the Reformational split. Catholics and Protestants tended to live in contiguous 'mutually exclusive' neighborhoods. His Catholic parents would not allow him to play with the children of his neighbors, because they were the children of a Protestant pastor. Later in life he berated the attitude of his parish priest in Schopfheim, Dr Arthur Steinman saying, "I cannot today sufficiently condemn it, but he had somehow equated 'anti-Protestant' with

---

2. From 1940, according to Swidler, Metzger gave Una Sancta talks to Catholic clergy, including in Stuttgart, Karlsruhe, Mannheim, Wiesbaden and Nuremburg, and gave lectures to Protestant and Catholic groups all over Germany. By the end of 1940 ecumenical circles had been founded in twenty-two cities across Germany. Swidler and O'Duffy *The Priest and the Führer*, 102.

# INTRODUCTION

'Catholic'. Perhaps it was necessary to emphasize the differences in order to secure thereby the faith consciousness of the diaspora congregation".[3] Max was, however, very adventurous and a little rebellious from childhood, pushing against such confessional boundaries and seeking to cross them and find out what was 'on the other side'. It was this same curiosity to cross boundaries which led him many years later—as a priest—to request and receive permission from his Bishop to attend the evangelical Lausanne *Faith and Order* Conference, in 1927. His heart was touched when he experienced the fellowship of other Christian believers both there and with the *International Fellowship of Reconciliation* (IFOR). At this time, such mixing with other Christians was indeed frowned upon, if not forbidden, in Germany and the worldwide Catholic Church. Such 'adventures' led him into a variety of ministries, including Temperance, and following a time as an army chaplain in World War I, into Peace work and finally to the quest for Christian Unity.

Though there were stirrings of ecumenical thinking in the Church in the early part of the 20th century, there was yet no ecumenical movement in Germany to gather up these tiny sparks into unity. Metzger decided that he would fan these sparks and little flames and attempt to create a powerful spiritual firestorm. He had, as we discussed earlier, little or no support from the Hierarchy, but his experiences in Meitingen in bringing Catholic clergy and Protestant pastors together taught him that that they had so much more in common than they had differences.

The title of this book is taken from the meeting in Dresden in 1941 where Metzger challenged his audience of 'all believing Christians' with the question of why Christians were still divided. In this, Metzger was certainly a voice in the wilderness of Nazi Germany, taking on waves of opposition, which eventually led to his execution and death at the age of 57, in Brandenburg Görden Prison in 1944. He had at most, lukewarm support from any church leader as he urged the churches to heed Jesus's prayer for unity given in John, Chapter 17—"that they may be one". With his innovative character and in the circumstances of WWII, he could not allow himself to take an easy road to be a quiet parish priest; he would offer himself, like his Lord, even to the death for his beliefs.

After his execution and the end of the War, the questions he had pondered in his life were taken up by others. It was said that Archbishop Jaeger didn't like the innovative experimental style or personality of Metzger,

3. Swidler and O'Duffy *The Priest and the Fuhrer*, 12

## Introduction

yet he decided to copy his model of the *Una Sancta Brotherhood* with the establishment of the *Adam Möhler Institute for Ecumenism* in Paderborn in 1946.[4] This development occurred just two years after the death of Metzger. This in turn led to the establishment of the Pontifical Secretariate and subsequent Pontifical Council for Christian Unity at the time of the Vatican Council, very much following the same lines etched out in Metzger's *Una Sancta Brotherhood*. We can trace the monumental achievement of the *Joint Declaration on the Doctrine of Justification* in 1999 right back to Metzger's work in Meitingen, Dresden and Berlin. However, we still must echo the same call and seek to answer the question today 'Why is there still no Christian Unity'? '

It is true that Catholic and Protestants globally are no longer distant from each other but have come much more into fellowship through such groups as the Charismatic Renewal movement, Emmaus, the Alpha Course and others. However, they are still divided in worship, practice and doctrine. The Western Church split after the failure of the Diet of Augsburg to bring together what were two groups of Catholic believers—traditional Catholics and the reformed Catholics of Luther. They had come together in 1530, to avoid a schism in the German Church. For many reasons which we will see, they failed to agree. Then the two sides started to drift further and further away from each other, into the situation like that which Metzger experienced as a child in Schopfheim, where he was not even allowed to play with local Protestant children. Metzger had studied enough to know this division of the Church in Germany was 'not of God' and was both bad and preventable at the time of Augsburg.[5] There was no defining issue or clearly formulated heresy to cause such a breakup of the church and so,—even before the epoch defining second Vatican Council,—he could ask the question 'Why is there *still* a separation of faith?' In many respects the same question undoubtedly still applies to us today.

---

4. Vereb Jerome-Michael C.P. *Because he was a German*, 105

5. See comments in Metzger's newspaper and Mission call of 1930 where he spoke of the ongoing fourth Centenary celebration happening, at the time of writing, in nearby Augsburg;

"I had to admit openly and freely that in the holy Church of God "in head and members" there was a lot that was rotten and annoying. And that therefore one in the reform movement should not simply be beaten with a club, but to be evaluated in the deepest sources—and to be appreciated. Well, unfortunately you can only learn one thing from history: people learn nothing from history." https://www.augsburg2030.org/augsburg-day-1930.html

INTRODUCTION

This book has a special aim which will become clearer as the argument unravels. The Catholic Church in Europe broke in two pieces following the failure of the Church authorities to accept the wording or immediately countenance the reforms suggested in the Lutheran '*Augsburg Confession*'. The disputants came very close to agreement, before the preventable split was seen in the seamless robe of Christ: the rent then widened and created numerous other rents and tears spreading over the next 400 and more years. In the 20th century, different church leaders, missionaries and authors started to plot a potential path of intellectual and spiritual return to unity through the ecumenical movement. Max Josef Metzger decided to pioneer that route in the difficult circumstances of Nazi Germany and to "run the race before him". Like his Lord, he was "surrounded by a great cloud of witnesses" and was prepared to throw off everything that entangled him that he might win the race, even to the point of his own martyrdom. (Hebrews 12:1–2)

We, too, are in the same relay race, and the baton now has been passed to us for our generation. So much of what apparently hindered Catholic–Lutheran division has successfully been analyzed, decided, and forensically removed. Whilst full unity might still be a distance from us, partial unity is possible in our lifetime, as we look to the 500th anniversary of the Augsburg Confession in 2030. Could it not be possible for both Catholics and Lutherans, without any major doctrinal compromise, to accept in some way the Articles of Melanchthon's Augsburg Confession? Thus, that first rent in the garment of Christ could be mended completely. As the first rent in 1530 meant many more tears in the garment, what might happen if this first rent is successfully mended? By God's grace it could mean the eventual restoration of the Christian unity that Jesus prayed for: "that we may be one".

January 1st 2025, South Carolina United States.

Further information on the path of reconcilation leading to 2030 can be found at **Augsburg2030.org**

# 1

# The Conversion of Luther

## IT ALL STARTED IN A TOWER

THERE WAS SOMETHING EXTRAORDINARY about the conversion of Martin Luther. Many others in history had found an experience of saving faith in the Gospel of Christ which changed them and re-directed their lives; we can think of Saint Catherine of Siena and Saint Anthony of Florence, Saint Thomas à Kempis or the Brethren of the Common life. Luther's conversion might have been more like that of St Paul,—utterly changing everything in his life.[1] Many know of the story of his becoming a monk and of his scrupulous life, where he sought by every means to 'gain' his salvation by a life of asceticism and rigorous devotion. He was, in many ways, terrified of God and his potential punishment if he failed, despite his dedication to his Christian path, to merit God's grace for life and life eternal. This was his life as a monk in the Augustinian Monastery in Wittenberg Germany. However,

---

1. It is interesting to compare the experience of Luther with St Paul. As a very zealous and well-educated Jewish radical, after his dramatic encounter with Christ on the way to Damascus, he did not go immediately to meet members of the Church in Jerusalem. Instead, according to Galatians 1:11–20, he "spent three years in Arabia." No account is given of what happened during this time. One can suggest he needed this time to make sense of his conversion in the light of his previous Jewish radical orthodoxy. We can perhaps think of the Young Luther being similar and, only after several years with the help of Melanchthon and others, having a more balanced orthodox theology which was then reflected in the Augsburg Confession.

as he poured over scripture in the monastery tower one night, it was as if a 'sudden light switched on' and he realized in reading Romans, that he could never merit the salvation of God; Jesus, by his death and Resurrection, had paid the price for his and all other's sins; all he needed to do was to trust and accept the gift. This message was not so much different from something an evangelist like Billy Graham might have said at any rally, drawing hundreds to receive that free gift of salvation. However, at this time in Germany, there were no such crusades or evangelistic outreaches; everyone was a nominal Christian,—at least by culture. Luther was essentially alone in his experience, and, with his uncompromising personality, he felt indeed that he had somehow managed to unlock the secret of the universe; his heart was thrilled with this experience of being 'born again'. He felt that the world, the church and all who would listen would have to change and find a similar personal relationship with God. He described it thus:

**Luther house Tower in Wittenberg**

Meanwhile in that same year, 1519, I had begun interpreting the Psalms once again. I felt confident that I was now more experienced, since I had dealt in university courses with St. Paul's Letters to the Romans, to the Galatians, and the Letter to the Hebrews. I had conceived a burning desire to understand what Paul meant in his Letter to the Romans, but thus far there had stood in my way, not the cold blood around my heart, but that one word which is in chapter one: "The justice of God is revealed in it." I hated that word, "justice of God," which, by the use and custom of all my teachers, I had been taught to understand philosophically as referring to formal or active justice, as they call it, i.e., that justice by which God is just and by which he punishes sinners and the unjust. But I, blameless monk that I was, felt that before God I was a sinner with an extremely troubled conscience. I couldn't be sure that God was appeased by my satisfaction. I did not love, no, rather I hated the just God who punishes sinners. In silence, if I did not blaspheme, then certainly I grumbled vehemently and got angry at God. I said, "Isn't it enough that we miserable sinners, lost for all eternity because of original sin, are oppressed by every kind of calamity through the Ten Commandments? Why does God heap sorrow upon sorrow through the Gospel and through the Gospel threaten us with his justice and his wrath?" This was how I was raging, with wild and disturbed conscience. I constantly badgered St. Paul about that spot in Romans 1 and anxiously wanted to know what he meant. I meditated night and day on those words until at last, by the mercy of God, I paid attention to their context: "The justice of God is revealed in it, as it is written: 'The just person lives by faith.'" I began to understand that in this verse the justice of God is that by which the just person lives by a gift of God, that is by faith. I began to understand that this verse means that the justice of God is revealed through the Gospel, but it is a passive justice, i.e. that by which the merciful God justifies us by faith, as it is written: "The just person lives by faith." All at once I felt that I had been born again and entered into paradise itself through open gates. Immediately I saw the whole of Scripture in a different light. I ran through the Scriptures from memory and found that other terms had analogous meanings, e.g., the work of God, that is, what God works in us; the power of God, by which he makes us powerful; the wisdom of God, by which he makes us wise; the strength of God, the salvation of God, the glory of God. I exalted this sweetest word of mine, "the justice of God," with as much love as before I had hated it with hate. This phrase of Paul was for me the very gate of paradise. Afterward I read Augustine's "On the Spirit and the Letter," in which I found what I had not dared hope for. I discovered that he too interpreted "the justice of God" in a similar way, namely, as that with which God clothes us when he justifies us. Although Augustine had said it imperfectly and did not explain in detail how God imputes justice to us, still it pleased me that he taught the justice of God by which we are justified."[2]

2. Thornton *Project Wittenberg* website

People often think of Luther as a great social and religious reformer. In many ways that is true, but it is all secondary to his own personal reformation which touched the deepest part of his powerful personality. He now interpreted everything he knew in the light of his experience and became increasingly disturbed by how he saw the world and the church; it seemed to miss the heart of the Gospel call to repentance. The Church indeed needed drastic reform; abuses were plenteous, from the Papal court to the local community, and the Church seemed to be more concerned with gaining wealth than in gaining and teaching souls. Lortz described the state of the Church in his epoch defining history of the Reformation—*The Reformation in Germany*:

> The call for a reformation in head and members was, to be sure, vastly different from a merely polemical antipapal or anti-Church movement. It was first of all the positive expression of the conviction which penetrated to the very roots of western consciousness that the profoundest order of the Church had become distorted, and which imperiously demanded a transformation; there was also the conviction that this transformation would come through a tremendous revolution an apocalyptic chastisement willed by God."[3]

The indulgences story is well- known, and Luther, the University teacher and theologian felt that people should consider this corruption. The famous couplet associated with Tetzel "As soon as a coin in the coffer rings, the soul from purgatory springs" summarized the belief of many with regard to the supposed benefit of the collection for indulgences. This was challenged in one of the 95 Theses he posted: "'They preach only human doctrines who say that as soon as the money clinks into the money chest, the soul flies out of purgatory."[4] Luther at this stage was acting like a good University class teacher wanting to expose corruption, and start a debate or discussion with students, but little did he know that his scholarly act in posting the Theses would impact all of Europe, reaching the Pope himself. As Lortz expounds about the impact of Luther on history: "The mighty change which the Reformation effected in the total life of Europe—ecclesiastical, religious, scientific, political and economic-was one half the result of a change and disintegration which set in around 1300. The other half was

---

3. Lortz, *The Reformation in Germany* Vol 1, 13. Lortz's two volume work gave for the first time a historically balanced unpolemical picture of the Reformation and a re-evaluation of the life and role of Luther.

4. Luther, 95 Theses, https://www.luther.de/en/95thesen.html

## The Conversion of Luther

Luther."⁵ When Luther was subsequently summoned to Leipzig to debate his propositions he was not going to compromise. Lortz describes the state of his mind:

> Luther was certainly also the spark that lit the heap of powder that had long been piling up, but he is much more. It seems easy to describe this man. His day-to-day life, outward and inward, is exposed to the clear light of day, as it were, in a great mass of his own sayings, and a colossal number of reports concerning him. His interior life, as we have said, was not exempt, for the amazing richness of his literary works—few of which should be described as 'books'—is one great confession of his agitated Soul."⁶

This was the powerful heart and troubled mind that was going to confront the medieval church now badly in need of a complete reform. Christopher Dawson described it thus:

> The hierarchical system of the medieval church had broken down, and no one was strong enough or courageous enough to carry out the drastic reforms that were necessary. Everyone was agreed in theory on the main evils: first, pluralism or the accumulation of ecclesiastical benefices in the hands of one man and the non-residence which was the direct result of this; secondly, simony or the dependence of ecclesiastical appointments and spiritual privileges on money; thirdly, the neglect of the canonical rule for episcopal visitations and diocesan synods; and fourthly, the low standard of clerical education and the religious ignorance of the laity.⁷

'Cometh the Hour, cometh the man'.⁸ Just as other figures in history were there at significant moments, so was Luther with all his complexity and stubbornness: hadn't God touched his life? He could not turn back to the ways he had known beforehand in the darkness of a troubled soul. "I can do no other" he said, unless he was persuaded by the same scriptures that had set him free from personal torment.⁹ It was as if a dam had been broken, with water flowing everywhere creating a flood, with Luther in its

---

5. Lortz, Reformation, 7–8
6. Lortz, Reformation, 167
7. Dawson, *The Dividing of Christendom*, 64
8. The phrase is said to derive from John 4;23 'But the hour cometh and now is.' It was also used of various historical figures such as British Winston Churchill and Jefferson Davis, President elect of the Confederacy.
9. Words spoken by Luther at the Diet of Worms in 1521 and considered a classical expression of personal freedom.

midst. Now he was viewed, not as a reformer, but as a heretic, and 'on the run' from the authorities of Church and State.

Chaos reigned, affecting the very heart of the Holy Roman Empire. Something had to happen to bring back a sense of order and to restore peace and unity. Finally, it was resolved to have a meeting regarding what had happened at Wittenberg and to consider what was new and seemingly divisive. Augsburg was chosen as place to bring peace, and Luther himself could not go to defend his ideas as he was on the run from authorities. Phillip Melanchthon instead went to represent the 'new teaching' of Luther in a scholarly fashion, as a mild-mannered layman, sharing it from the heart of Christian revelation and Church teaching.[10] It was not really anything completely new on which he expounded, but something that had been missing in the corruption and lukewarmness of the medieval church,—the question of a personal return to Christ by the individual. The whole edifice of Christianity had to be built on this foundation—none other than Christ who was the founder and foundation of the faith itself. Despite Melanchthon's gentle means of persuasion and his highly orthodox Catholic- based Augsburg Confession, no concordance developed between the delegates.

One could look at these events spiritually and suggest that the devil himself was out to twist everything out of all proportion, and to wreck the chance of genuine reform happening to Church and State. The meeting itself was thus a failure; the sides could not meet and the attempt at agreement was abandoned—the promise was left unfulfilled. Nothing like this was ever intended by Luther or Melanchthon: it was like an abrupt unexpected divorce, where partners had to pick up the pieces of an ungodly fracas. Much bitterness was found, especially with those who were wishing for reform. Led by Luther, the reformers were still convinced of the need to return to the roots of the Gospel, to clear teaching and proper practice. However, like partners arguing in an acrimonious divorce, the two sides started to drift further and further apart from each other, with the Reformers bringing with them, not just individual churches, but nations. Within a period of time, many of the abuses that Luther had seen were addressed by the Church in the Council of Trent, but it was too late: there were now

---

10. Phillip Melanchthon (1497–1560) was a German collaborator of Luther and the first systematic Theologian of the Protestant Reformation. Moderately unknown relative to Luther, his house still stands as a museum in Wittenberg. Unlike the Luther House nearby, however it receives hardly any visitors. It can however be argued that his work created the foundation of the modern Lutheran denomination through his writing of the Confessional statement, the Augsburg Confession.

several independent churches in Europe, divided from Rome, seeking to have an independent Church life.

- How are we now 500 years later?
- Have we managed to heal the schism?
- Is it still too wide?

One is reminded of Joseph and his brothers in Genesis. When they met in Egypt, they did not recognize each other as being from the same family and it required a moment of revelation for them to recognize each other and be healed. That division lasted a lifetime: the division of Christians is now sadly almost 500 years old, but things have been happening in the past century to help with this recognition.

Picture from 1945 of Prisoners being released from the Priest's Block at Dachau Concentration Camp. Among the over 2700 clergy imprisoned in the camp were 2227 Catholic priests and religious and 109 Protestant clergy. 117 of the Catholic clergy were subsequently named 'Blessed' or Saints by the Church. Among the Protestant pastors imprisoned were Rev. Martin Niemöller and Rev. Max Lackmann. (cf.ch.10) Notice the triangular symbol on the central figure with the letter 'P' on his shirt, indicating the German word *Priester* or priest.

One of the greatest things—whilst perhaps also the saddest things- was the joint experience of Catholic and Protestant priests and pastors in the time of the Second World War in Germany. In the heart of concentration camps, pastors and priests did recognize each other as brothers in Christ with the same faith; more than anything the common suffering for the Gospel promoted a gradual return to fellowship and unity in the whole body of Christ. With hard work, agreement was achieved about the issue that changed Luther. In 1999 the *Joint Declaration on the Doctrine of Justification* (JDDJ) declared in simple words that the World Lutheran Federation and the Roman Catholic Church agreed on the meaning of the words "Justification by faith". Following this agreement, other parts of the divided body of Christ started to join the long road towards unity, with Anglican, Methodist and Reformed Churches agreeing to the Declaration. The Churches were not thus unified, but they were no longer separated; much more now needs to happen to bring them closer together.

As we approach the 500th anniversary of the writing of the Confession in 2030, it would seem to be important to gain a reconciled agreement between the churches on the Articles of the Augsburg Confession. The Confession became the foundational document of the worldwide "Lutheran" Communion. As we shall see, agreement nearly happened between the Church and the Reformers in 1530: it was so close: Could it happen 500 years later in 2030?

This is our prayer.

# 2

# The Relevance of the Augsburg Confession Today

MANY PEOPLE LOOKING AT the largely divided state of Christianity today, and indeed for the last 500 years, would tend to blame it on the life and protests of Augustinian German monk Fr. Martin Luther, who nailed his 95 theses to the church of All Saints in the small University town of Wittenberg in 1519. While Luther was indeed the spark of the Reformation in Germany in those times, he cannot be said to be the author of the division in Christianity that happened at that time. If one wants to understand where the division occurred, and undoubtedly where it needs to be healed, one needs to look at the events of 1530 in the City of Augsburg and the creation of what was called the *Augsburg Confession*.[1] It was the failure to agree on this confession of evangelical faith that initially ushered in two different churches in Germany, and, following this, the creation of many national churches and denominations across Europe who were no longer attached to the Church of Rome.

- What was this Confession and who wrote it?
- Why was it not accepted, or could it have been accepted at the time, as it was?

1. The Augsburg Confession also known in Latin as the *Confessio Augustana* or in this text shortened to "CA".

- Was it viewed as heretical?
- Why did it not perhaps usher in a peaceful reformation of the Catholic Church in the light of the abuses of the time?
- Can it be revived and agreed on today?
- Why should Catholics and Lutherans of today take an interest in this forgotten piece of history?

We will try to examine these questions in this time leading up to the 500th anniversary of its creation in June 2030.

From the time of Luther, the German church was in a state of confusion over doctrine and practice. The scandal of the selling of indulgences was in the air and beliefs were in a state of flux concerning Christianity itself and the questions of salvation: what must one do to be saved? At the center of the drama was Luther who had been declared a heretic and had taken his stand at the Diet of Worms, with his most famous saying "I cannot and will not recant. I cannot do otherwise. Here I stand. God help me. Amen." Splits were beginning to show in the unity of the Church with arguments about the Real Presence in the Eucharist and the question of infant baptism, issues where Luther adhered to the traditional teaching of the Catholic Church. The divisions worried the political order with disunity in Germany making it harder to confront the invading Turks who had already reached the gates of Vienna. To restore order and bring civil, as well as religious calm and peace, the Imperial Diet of Nurnberg was given notice that there would be an assembly gathered to discuss all these controversies, clarify all these doctrinal issues and bring some unity. They were hoping that kindness and reason—if not, then possible threats—could bring an end to the disturbances and unite the Empire. The Emperor, Charles V, invited all the princes of the German speaking territories to a national assembly to be held in the City of Augsburg in June 1530. The delegation of theologians from the University of Wittenberg, where Luther taught, were under the leadership of the mild-mannered Phillip Melanchthon. He was given the responsibility by the territorial princes to rework a Saxon Confession into a common Evangelical Confession that could be presented to the Emperor. Preliminary drafts were made before they were presented for approval by the Princes of Saxony, Braunschweig, Brandenburg, Hesse, Lüneburg, and Saxon Anhalt.

# The Relevance of the Augsburg Confession Today

## THE AUGSBURG CONFESSION JUNE 25TH, 1530

The reading itself was due to take place in the Chapter Room of the Episcopal Palace in Augsburg. On Saturday, June 25th 1530, at three o clock in the afternoon the Chancellor, Dr Christian Beyer, stood up and walked towards the Emperor of the Holy Roman Empire. 200 people were present to listen in addition to a large crowd gathered in the courtyard outside. The Chancellor initially started to read the Confession in German while Dr. Brück held the Latin version aloft. After the reading, the German princes present stood to show their support for the Confession. Dr. Brück then took the Latin and German copies of the Confession and presented them to the Emperor. It is reported that he then announced: "Most gracious Emperor, this is a Confession that will even prevail against the gates of Hell, with the grace and help from God."[2]

Prior to the events at Augsburg, German priest and theologian, Johann Eck, had prepared a highly inaccurate account of Luther and his attempt at Church reform. Though initially friendly to Luther, Eck had been to Rome and had helped to create the document *Exurge Domini*, which was a Bill of Excommunication for Luther. To cast him as a heretic, he had prepared a lengthy attack on the Reformer and those who followed him, called *Four Hundred and Four articles for the Diet of Augsburg*. He stated that Luther wished to change doctrines to those which were being proclaimed by the radical Anabaptists and Zwinglians. In so doing, he was trying to prove that Luther, and his reform was not in line with historical Christianity. The Augsburg Confession, however, was written to show the Catholic nature of the Reform which indeed held to Catholic Christian traditional beliefs.

Following the presentation of the Confession, the Roman leaders met in discussion for the following days of June 26–27, and then presented the Emperor with a report asking for a response to Melanchthon's Confession. Within a space of five weeks a *Confutation* (a refutation or rebuttal of the Confession) was composed by the same John Eck (who had already designated Luther as a heretic) together with John Faber, Konrad Wimpina and the biographer and nemesis of Luther, Fr. John Cochlaeus. Their report amounted to 280 pages. The Emperor ordered the writers to moderate their tone and responses and to condense the documents. After five attempts and six weeks effort, the Confutation was finally reduced to twelve pages and was then read out in the same chamber room of the Episcopal Palace on

---

2. Melanchthon *The Augsburg Confession* .9

August 3rd. Like the Confession, it was prepared in both languages of Latin and German and read out in German. The Reformers were not, however, given an opportunity to respond, and thus asked to have a copy of the Confutation. They were told they could only have a copy on three conditions:

- Firstly, that they did not respond to its critique in writing.
- Secondly, that they neither printed it nor publicized it in any way.
- Thirdly, that they had to rejoin the Empire and the Catholic Estates and concur with the Confutation on every point.

It was to be regarded as the end of this subject and the unchallenged final word on the question of Church Reform. The demands were not accepted by the Reformers, and they were consequently not given a copy of the text.

While Melanchthon was not present for the reading of the *Confutation*, scribes had, in fact, written down the text of the Confutation during the rebuttal. This gave the possibility of a 'rebuttal of the rebuttal'. Phillip Melanchthon thus spent the following six weeks writing a lengthy *Apology* explaining, in greater detail, all the points that he had made in the Confession. It was the position also that was accepted by Luther himself, who said:

"I have read over Master Phillip's Apologia; it pleases me very much and I don't know how to improve it or change it. Nor would it be suitable, since I cannot tread so gently and lightly. Christ our Lord grant that it will bear much fruit, as we hope and ask. Amen."

He was, however, disappointed.

Melanchthon presented the Apologia to the Emperor on September 22nd. It was received by the Count Palatinate Frederick on behalf of the Emperor, but was quickly returned unread, or not to be considered by the Emperor. By refusing the countenance of the *Apology* and reopening the debate, one might conclude that with the failure to agree, the first serious cracks of division appeared in the unified walls of the Church. A split occurred that continued to affect Church unity for the next 500 years until the present day. The two sides retreated from each other, like members of a family that suffer avoidable estrangement. The Council of Trent, for its part, did not discuss the *Augsburg Confession* or the *Apologia*. Instead, polemically exaggerated statements of Luther and the Reformers were gathered together in volumes which were then regarded as heretical. Even though many of these statements had been corrected in the Augsburg Confession, they were then used as the theological substance of the Evangelical church, and the

# The Relevance of the Augsburg Confession Today

revised Evangelical position in the Confession did not enter the picture. Other unfortunate events helped to color the Catholic understanding of the Reform movement. There were attacks on statues and monasteries and some priests were stoned at the pulpit by those adhering to the new teachings. Some were hounded by mobs and banished from their cities. This did not help opponents of Luther to see the Reformation with the same eyes.

At a convocation at Schweinfurt in 1532, Church leaders of Hesse, Strasbourg, Liegnitz, Pomerania, Hanover and Halle bound all their pastors to teach in accordance with the Augsburg Confession. Very quickly the teaching of the CA spread until finally, in its unaltered form, it became part of the *Book of Concord*– the basic collection of Lutheran Confessions brought together in Dresden in 1580. This had now become the textbook of Lutheran Congregations. Politically Germany continued to split into different confessional states, Catholic and Lutheran. At the Peace of Augsburg on September 29th, 1555, a law was proclaimed to allow each state to choose its own confession with the idea 'whose land—whose religion' (*Cuius regio, eius religio*). Much animosity continued for centuries between the members of the different states. The Thirty years War itself was very much fought on confessional lines.

- Was it all necessary? Could it all have been avoided? Were the two paths completely divergent? Was there no possibility of any compromise?
- Could one say that the gathering was biased against the Reformers, not giving them a fair and reasonable trial? Luther wrote after the Diet of Augsburg, "I fear that we will never again get as close together as we did at Augsburg."

Over 100 years later, in 1687, a French Jesuit Fr. Jean Dez attempted to make such an accommodation between the two sides of the debate. He wrote a commentary on the *Augsburg Confession* called *Reunion of the Protestants of Strasbourg with the Roman Church which is necessary for their salvation and easy according to their doctrine*. He wrote it as an imagined dialogue between Catholics and Lutherans, and carefully examined the 28 articles of the Confession, including all the objections of Roman Catholics and Protestants. It was published in France in 1687, and then in Germany a year later. He concluded that the doctrinal content of the CA and Melanchthon's Apology would make a return and reunification of the Churches both "necessary and easy."[3] What in fact happened in the ensuing years

---

3. Lackmann, *Augsburg Confession*, 33.

was that Catholics now viewed individual Protestants as possible targets of missionary activity: each one had to be 'reconverted' to the 'One True Faith.' The Protestant, in his turn, no longer belonged to this Church, and thus he no longer listened to it, and regarded it as his antithesis. Max Lackmann, Lutheran Pastor and notable post war ecumenist said, "This method of confrontation is extraordinarily comfortable, except that it is not true, not responsible to the Holy Spirit and to the heritage of the Church's history and is therefore absolutely hopeless."[4]

Since the Vatican Council there has been renewed interest in what did and did not happen at the time of the Augsburg Confession. In the much-improved atmosphere between the churches which led to the *Joint Declaration on the Doctrine of Justification* in 1999, working groups of Lutherans and Catholics have been reexamining both the content and circumstances of the writing of the Augsburg Confession. The Diocesan Commission of Münster in Germany, took up the question again in 1974 and declared:

> The German Conference of Bishops might examine the possibility of the Catholic Church recognizing the Augsburg Confession. Such a recognition would, first, take the CA seriously in its historical and contemporary significance as an expression of Protestant-Lutheran faith; at the same time, it would dismantle a Catholic view of Lutheranism which is determined above all by polemically exaggerated Reformation expressions. . . Secondly such a recognition would be an acknowledgement that the CA advocates no Church dividing teachings and that it can be affirmed on the Catholic side as a witness to the faith of the Church universal.[5]

Vinzenz Pfnür (1937–2012) Catholic Theologian and author, in a book of essays entitled *The Role of the Augsburg Confession*, explained how jaundiced views of the Reformation and of Luther have become normative in Catholic books of Church history. While they include statements of Luther from his early years of "joy, freedom and exaggeration," no mention is ever given to the gentle irenic statements of reform in the Augsburg Confession. Despite the work of scholars such as Joesph Lortz (1887–1975) to rectify some of the exaggerated images of the early Reformation, the standard Catholic polemic against Luther, by Cochläeus, had prevailed. Pfnür says, in contrast

---

4. Lackmann, *Augsburg Confession*.33

5. Burgess, *The Role of the Augsburg Confession*, 4 quoting KNA—Ökumenische Information , No 6 Feb 1974 10–11

to the early Reformation writings of Luther and Melanchthon, the Augsburg Confession "was not viewed as a full expression of Protestant view."[6]

The background to the CA was indeed turbulent. Many voices were being raised in protest politically and religiously, waiting to be heard. Luther was the religious symbol at the center of this time, influencing all branches of Germany society, including the knights, peasants, princes and the Imperial Cities. Religious views ranged from the apocalyptic Thomas Müntzer to various other groups of enthusiasts, the Anabaptists and Huldrych Zwingli. There came a time for polemics to cease and to distill what was essentially Christian in all this tumult. This was the purpose of the Augsburg Confession. In concluding the initial 21 Articles, Melanchthon wrote, given here in a new translation by Robert Kolb and Timothy Wengert:

> This is nearly a complete summary of what is preached and taught in our churches for proper Christian instruction and the comfort of consciences, as well as for the improvement of believers. For we certainly wish neither to expose our own souls and consciences to grave danger before God by misusing the divine name or Word nor to pass on or bequeath to our children and descendants any other teaching than that which accords with the pure Word of God and Christian truth. Since, then, this teaching is clearly grounded in Holy Scripture and is, moreover, neither against nor contrary to the universal Christian church—or even the Roman church—so far as can be observed in the writings of the Fathers, we think that our opponents cannot disagree with us in the articles set forth above. That is why those who undertake to isolate, reject, and avoid our people as heretics, without having themselves any solid basis in divine command or Scripture, act in a very unfriendly and hasty manner, contrary to all Christian unity and love. For the dissension and quarrel are chiefly over some traditions and abuses. Since then, there is nothing unfounded or deficient in the principal articles and since this our confession is godly and Christian, the bishops should in all fairness act more leniently even if there were a deficiency in regard to tradition—although we hope to offer solid grounds and reasons why some traditions and abuses have been changed among us.[7]

Having a literary scholarly exposition of official theological beliefs put the Augsburg Confession in a class of its own in a time of great conflict and

---

6. Burgess, *The Role of the Augsburg Confession* 5.

7. Robert Kolb and Timothy Wengert *The Book of Concord A New Translation, Augsburg Confession*,58.

confusion. It was one achievement to distill the ideas of the Reformation into a Confession of 28 Articles; it was quite another thing to have them accepted at Augsburg.

# 3

# The Historical Records of the Augsburg Confession

TRYING TO UNDERSTAND ALL the complex history of the writing of the Augsburg Confession in 1530 poses many difficulties historically. There are only two clear accessible historical records of the Diet which themselves are both problematic. The first is contained in a biography of Luther by Johannes Cochlaeus entitled *Commentaria de'Actis et scriptis Martini Lutheri*. This was the principle Catholic record of Luther's life published in Latin in Mainz in 1549. It is the fullest eyewitness account of the life of Luther with more than 175,000 words and gives a vivid description of the events at the Diet of Augsburg. Cochlaeus (1479-1552) was an ordained Catholic priest who was extremely conservative and regarded himself as one of the main critics of the work and writing of Martin Luther. After Luther was excommunicated for his writing on January 1521, Cochlaeus was present at the Diet of Worms where Luther sought to defend his beliefs and made his famous statement: "Here I stand. I can do no other". Subsequently, Cochlaeus got to know Luther personally and debated with him. He attended the Augsburg Diet in 1530 where he had an official role and described the Diet in detail in his biography of Luther. Because of Cochlaeus's great antagonism for the Reformation, and his often brazen unabashed accounts of Luther, his ideas and ideals and those of the other reformers, his Latin account remained untranslated for over 450 years.

Cochlaeus account was thus only published for the first time in English in 2002 in a book called *Luther's Lives*[1]. This included both Melanchthon's Life of Luther and the account of Cochlaeus. While undoubtedly his work influenced many scholars of Latin in this time, his work was inaccessible for many until quite recently. Melanchthon's more sympathetic eyewitness life of Luther, however, finished with the events of 1521, nine years before the Diet of Augsburg itself took place.

According to Professor Robert Kolb of Concordia Lutheran Seminary, the only account of the Augsburg Confession and Diet from a more Lutheran perspective was that of the former secretary of Frederick the Wise, Georg Spalatin (1484–1545). He was present at the Diet and wrote an account of the time in Latin that was in manuscript form and then was only printed 300 years later in the 18th century. This manuscript seems to have been the source of an account in a book in 1867 written by German Lutheran theologian, Gustav Leopold Plitt (1835–1880), entitled *Einleitung in die Augustana*. We are not sure of any other possible accounts of the Diet that have been made. Plitt fills in many of the details which were not in the narrative of Cochlaeus. It has rarely been published in English with the first being in a book by Johann Michael Reu called *The Augsburg Confession: A Collection of sources* published in 1930. Up to that time all the relevant documents covering the Diet were written in German and Latin and were widely scattered in different sources and publications that had appeared from 1730–1930. They had never been gathered, and only one third had been available in English. Reu was the first one to make them accessible in English in 1930, on the 400th anniversary of the Confession.[2] This in turn was more recently published in *Sources and Contexts of the Book of Concord* in 2001, with some parts translated on the Concordia Seminary University website in St Louis. Taken together with Cochlaeus' description, we may have a better understanding of the controversial events at Augsburg. In reading them together, we may perhaps better understand some of the reasons why the Diet did not solve the 'religious question' in Germany which, in turn, led to the schism of a large section of the Western Church. Both accounts miss details which may not have suited the argument from one position or another.

---

1. Vandiver, Elizabeth Keen Ralph and Frazel Thomas D. Luther's Lives: Two contemporary accounts of Martin Luther Manchester University Press Manchester and NY 2002

2. Reu, *The Augsburg Confession*, introduction.

What is very surprising is that the possibility of any objective examination in any way of all the elements (excluding Latin texts) that went into the creation of the schism in Western Christianity has only really been possible in a relatively recent period in the 21st century, nearly 500 years after the events themselves! It would seem that neither account of the Diet of Augsburg was completely objective. Indeed, the two accounts of the time, which were in virtual opposition to each other, were largely accepted and believed by both sides of the schism, from the 16th century until the 20th century. Through the work of Lortz[3] and others, both Catholics and Lutherans, we now have a more objective and sympathetic view of the life and teaching of Luther himself, but one could suggest the two parts of the Churches of the Reformation have not as yet come to an objective understanding of what actually caused them to separate at the time of the Augsburg Confession. Neither have we considered if that schism could have been addressed more equitably in any way and perhaps have been healed. What is described in the next chapters is an attempt to draw on both narratives together with some descriptions of these events by Cochlaeus, the accounts derived from Plitt and Reu and the texts available on the Concordia University website[4].

## THE BACKGROUND IN EUROPE IN 1530

In the mid-16th century Europe was in turmoil; the Turks were advancing throughout the Holy Roman Empire and were closing in on the city of Vienna. The Emperor was concerned with the lack of unity that had developed in Germany following Luther's protest over corruption in the Church and the controversy of the sale of indulgences. Dissention was rife. To quell the social and religious storms in the light of an invasion of Europe by the Turkish Army, he decided to call a meeting—or a 'Diet'- in the German City of Augsburg in Bavaria. The purpose was twofold: to discuss a method of defeating the advancing Turkish army, and to seek to abolish all discord in matters of religious faith and practice that had arisen. On March 11th, 1539, an Edict (or summons) was sent from the Emperor to the Electoral Duke of Saxony, where religious dissent had started. The summons stated:

> ...how in the matter of errors and divisions concerning the holy faith and the Christian religion we may and should deal and

3. Lortz Joseph *Die Reformation in Deutschland* The Reformation in Germany English Trans. Darton Longman and Todd 1939

4. https://bookofconcord.org/other-resources/sources-and-context

> resolve. and so bring it about, in better and sounder fashion, that divisions may be allayed, antipathies set aside, all past errors left to the judgment of our Savior, and *every care taken to give a charitable hearing to every man's opinion, thoughts, and notions, to understand them, to weigh them, to bring and reconcile them to a unity in Christian truth,* to dispose of everything that has not been rightly explained or treated of on the one side or the other, to see to it that one single, true religion may be accepted and held by us all and that we all live in one common church and unity.[5]

The Emperor seemed to be sincere in his aim to have open discussion of all the religious difficulties that had presented themselves in the different states, which he felt should no longer be ignored. He, himself, was in favor of a general Christian Council,—as were the Reformers,—such as had happened in other centuries to help address abuses and possible heresy. He had confidence that his efforts would be successful, and the recent benediction of the Pope encouraged him to believe in his mission.[6] Reu describes his motivation thus:

> Every single estate was to be heard and given an opportunity to voice its opinion, thoughts and ideas. Evidently the Emperor did not care to deal with a larger group such as had come together in signing the Protest at Speyer. He intended to recognize only individual independent princes and cities who would be able to inform him regarding the actual conditions in the churches of their own domain. In this way he hoped to gain an insight into their doctrine, their innovations, their whole ecclesiastical outlook, and to make practical use of this information; to keep the separate cities apart, to make more acute their differences, especially those concerning the doctrine of the Sacrament, and so nip in the bud every effort to form a party."[7]

Immediately, John, the Elector of Saxony, made plans to attend the Diet together with his Chancellor Dr. George Bruck. As religious opinions were to be discussed, the Elector wrote to the theologians at the University of Wittenberg in central Saxony, and namely to Martin Luther, Justin Jonas, Bugenhagen and Phillip Melanchthon. He asked them to prepare a memorandum on the religious issues which were causing dissention in the State. Other German States and religious groups, such as the Zwinglians in

---

5. Reu, *A Collection of Sources*, 38 (Author's italics)
6. Reu.41
7. Reu.42

## The Historical Records of the Augsburg Confession

Zürich, were also being summoned with a hope to reach a broad agreement on all religious matters. They were instructed as described in the book of Pliff and translated by Concordia:

> Since among the subjects to be discussed, [he says] one is with respect to the dissension concerning our Christian Religion, it is important that a statement or opinion be first discussed and determined among the States themselves, [including] the matters both in faith and in outward Church ceremonies concerning which there is dissent. In this way, before the Diet begins a decision may be reached as to how far we and the other States that have received the pure doctrine can with a good conscience endure prevalent abuses.[8]

The theologians of Wittenberg were asked to complete their memorandum and to bring it to the Elector of the city of Torgau who would then bring it to the 'Diet' at Augsburg. On route to the Diet, they received further instructions, asking not just for a statement of abuses, but also for a positive doctrinal statement of Christian faith. The idea of this document was to repudiate certain extreme groups that had been vocal at the time. Phillip Melanchthon thus prepared what he called an *exordium* or a list of doctrinal statements which would precede the enumeration of abuses which they sought to have addressed.

Preparations were already at hand in Augsburg for the arrival of the Emperor. The event was to be well attended and historical, with great joy and splendor. Cardinals and Archbishops from the region had all been summoned, with many princes and nobility from the regions. The Emperor himself was due to be greeted by Lord Christopher of Stadion, the Bishop of Augsburg. When the Emperor arrived, he was escorted to the Cathedral Church for a ceremony of blessing, concluding with the singing of *Te Deum Laudamus*. As it was the Feast of Corpus Christi the following day the Emperor requested that all,—including the Lutherans,—join the public procession to celebrate the feast where the Sacrament of the Body of Christ was to be displayed, carried and honored. Cochlaeus relates that the Lutherans declined to attend "claiming obstacles to faith in this matter."[9] The procession proceeded without them, with the secular princes, Masters of the Curia, the Primate of Germany and many nobles and electors, with "musicians of different sorts singing praises to God." Cochlaeus relates that

---

8. Book of Concord https://bookofconcord.org/other-resources/sources-and-context/johann-eck-404-theses/ Introduction Accessed 11/15/23

9. Vandiver, *Luther's lives*, 248

the non-attendance and "stubbornness" of the Lutherans caused the Emperor "much distress" and that he wished them to depart from the Diet the following day without being heard. Cochlaeus relates that other princes "begged His Majesty to sooth his anger and give them an audience." The Emperor agreed and the Lutherans then joined the rest of the procession for Mass the following day at the Cathedral.[10]

Tempers had flared it would seem. Why incident might have occured one might ask? Was it just a conscience matter, or were there other factors at work?

During the first week of the arrival of the Lutherans in Augsburg, they found that they had been preceded, amongst others, by a Professor of Theology from Ingolstadt. He was Johann Meier von Eck and known as Dr. John Eck. He was formerly friendly with Martin Luther but had fallen out with him following the publication of the XCV Theses. They had faced each other at the Leipzig debate in 1519, which had resulted in Luther being threatened with excommunication by Pope Leo X in the Papal Bull, *Exurge Domini*.[11] In 1520, Eck went to Rome and helped in writing the Bull which then caused Luther's excommunication.[12] He thus portrayed himself as the primary supporter of the Pope in Germany and had therefore become an indefatigable opponent of the work of Martin Luther. Before the commencement of the Diet and the arrival of the representatives of the states, he had composed and printed a pamphlet of thirty-four pages, giving his views on the reformers and the work of Luther. This pamphlet had already been in circulation and on sale in Augsburg for some period before the arrival of Melanchthon and the Reformers. The title read:

> Under the Patronage of the Lord Jesus and Mary. Four Hundred and Four Articles; Some pertaining to the Disputations at Leipzig, Baden, and Berne; others drawn from the writings of those disturbing the peace of the Church; which John Eck, the very least minister of the Church, offers to discuss before the Emperor Charles V. and the Princes of the Empire, as is explained more at large in the program at Augsburg; on a day and hour to be hereafter published by consent of the Emperor.[13]

10. Vandiver *Luther's Lives*, 248

11. https://en.wikipedia.org/wiki/Leipzig_Debate

12. Rosin, Robert Sources and Contexts of the Book of Concord (Minneapolis: Fortress 2001.from Email conversation with Professor Kolb

13. Reu *A Collection of Sources*, 99 Latin Translated by Henry Eyster Jacobs Dean of Evangelical Lutheran Seminary Philadelphia. 1908 https://bookofconcord.org/

# The Historical Records of the Augsburg Confession

In his cover letter to Charles V, Johann Eck writes the following which needs to be quoted in full:

> Most Revered Emperor: By all Catholics, thou art esteemed as one who has been appointed, elected, and consecrated of God to come to the aid of the wavering catholic faith, to help the afflicted Church and oppressed churchmen, to maintain the Christian State against the sanguinary Turkish tyrant, the Sultan, and, in a word, to save the Christian world. But since Martin Luther, a domestic enemy of the Church, has not been improved by the former admonition of Thy Imperial Majesty, but having fallen into every Scylla and Charybdis of impiety, calls the Pope of Rome Antichrist; the Church a harlot ; bishops, masques and idols ; universities, synagogues of Satan; cloisters, brothels; theologians, bats; secular princes, fools, drunkards, insane, and worse than Turks; and meanwhile does not withhold himself from attacks also upon Thy Holy Majesty, but teaches the lordship of Christ and maligns and ridicules Thy Imperial mandates with the most obscene interpretations. And since, also, he has reached such an extremity of desperation, as a blasphemer of God, impious towards the saints and sacraments, irreverent, reproachful, and rebellious towards all superiors, ecclesiastical as well as secular, an enemy of all good men, that he praises none but heretics, extols schismatics, excites seditions in Germany, prepares for shedding a flood of Christian blood, and is collecting bands of Germans to bathe themselves in the blood of the Pope and his Cardinals, and is producing a generation of vipers still worse than himself—for to Luther we owe as his children the iconoclasts, Sacramentarians, Capernaites, new Hussites and their progeny the Anabaptists, the new Epicureans who deny the immortality of the soul, and the spiritualists as well as the new Corinthians who deny the divinity of Christ.
>
> Since also they are rending Germany with these monstrosities and portents, demolishing churches, overthrowing altars, treading underfoot the most holy Eucharist, burning the images of Christ and the saints, abolishing divine worship, casting the images of saints into the rubbish heaps, raging against the gold and silver treasures of the Church, despoiling the revenues of churches and monasteries, voiding the last wills and testaments of the deceased, and, in short, attacking all things pertaining to the Christian religion even worse than Turks, so as by their persecutions and threats to induce virgins consecrated to God to abandon the cloisters; very many of them, amidst crimes so execrable, even

---

other-resources/sources-and-context/johann-eck-404-theses/

dare to announce their readiness to defend themselves according to the Recess of the Diet of Spires, and to respond concerning these things to God and thy Most August Majesty, as though thou art a patron of their impieties, blasphemies, thefts, sacrileges, and seditions, pretending that the most holy Imperial Head of the world, and hoping that the supreme justice of the divine Emperor, would defend their supreme injustice. Notwithstanding the unlawfulness of agitating and discussing anew the things rightly judged and arranged by a Council, they excite ancient heresies condemned more than a thousand years ago, follow teachers who have been burned, and men of accursed memory, seducing simple people with the plea that they follow the Gospel, the Bible, the Word of God. I offer myself, therefore, to Thy Imperial Majesty, prepared, as at Leipzig against Luther, and at Baden against Oecolampadius,[14] to repel their mendacious boasts, to defend all the institutions, practices, doctrines, and observances of the Catholic faith, and to attack their assailants. Let the Church's enemies, the ministers of ungodliness, the patrons of heresies, the vessels of iniquity, come forth and fulfill that whereof they so insolently boast to the people; let them answer concerning the faith before the Power which is of God, the Member of God, the Church's Advocate, the faith's Protector.

Farewell, Father of the country, Most August and Victorious Emperor. God protect and guide thee; grant thee victory over the Turk, and mercifully extend thy rule still farther. "[15]

It is perhaps not surprising that this letter was neither quoted nor referred to in the Book by Cochleaus. Its pointed negativity and exaggerated content would not have sounded fair or balanced to Cochlaeus' readers. It is also quite remarkable to find that such a pamphlet against Luther and the evangelicals was circulated at the time, has largely been unavailable in modern Lutheran books about the Augsburg Confession in English. It is not given in *Concordia* the *Readers Book of the Lutheran Confessions— The Lutheran Confession* published in 2001, nor the smaller *The Augsburg Confession the Concordia Reader's edition* used for study in American Lutheran Churches[16]. The times indeed were turbulent, but one would be hard

---

14. Oecolampadius (1482—24 November 1531) was a German Protestant reformer in the Calvinist tradition from the Electoral Palatinate. https://en.wikipedia.org/wiki/Johannes_Oecolampadius

15. Reu, *A Collection of Sources*, 97–99.

16. *Concordia The Lutheran Confessions* Concordia St Louis 2005. The Augsburg Confession Readers Edition 2005

# The Historical Records of the Augsburg Confession

pressed not to say that the wording was highly offensive and out of line with any sense of Christian charity. It would seem to create prejudice or poison in the minds of the Emperor and those who would hear the Confession of Melanchthon, and to state beforehand that no compromise could be created with any of the Reformer's ideas.

Before the commencement of the Diet, Melanchthon sought to explain to Luther what had eventuated in Augsburg, detailing the need for a proper Confession of faith. "For this purpose, I have embraced all the articles of faith, because Eck has published against us the most diabolical slanders."[17] His inclusion of the doctrinal articles of the Augsburg Confession were his 'remedy'. He felt that this was most important, given the spread of the assertions of the 404 theses which had been circulating around the population of Augsburg. Melanchthon's purpose was to clear the air from any misconceptions that Emperor might have had, having heard Eck's propositions with an almost 'academic' statement description of Lutheran faith and understanding and some abuses which needed to be addressed. The idea was to declare,—without a dialectic on the misrepresentations of Eck and the question of their veracity,—a statement 'taking higher ground' on all subject matters for which the Lutherans felt responsible. He sent an early draft of the Confession to Luther who spent the whole time of the Diet in nearby Coburg. Luther remarked on reading the draft: "It pleases me quite well and I know nothing to improve or change in it, nor would it work if I did, since I cannot step so gently and softly."[18] Luther recognized that Melanchthon's diplomacy and erudition might perhaps win the day where perhaps Luther's more powerful character and speech might have proven to be combustible in such circumstances.

Where did Eck draw all his material to denigrate the Evangelicals? Reu describes it thus:

> As early as July 4, 1524, while at the Regensburg Convent, he had already sent a request to the senate of the Vienna University asking the four faculties to prepare in all haste a compendium which would afford a complete insight in the heretical writings and innovations in the faith recently circulated among the people. Ferdinand came back to this idea in January 1530. In his mandate of January 12, to the members of the Collegium Archducal in Vienna, "he demanded that they were first to examine Luther's

---

17. Book of Concord Website.404-theses/introduction/

18. *Concordia Theological Quarterly* http://www.ctsfw.net/media/pdfs/klugluther-scontribution.pdf 158

writings but were also to arrange carefully, with notations as to sources, all the others of the last twelve years, together with all the old and new heresies, changes in the sacraments and ecclesiastical order," seditious speeches, invectives, and other errors, in a summary. This was to be in his hands by the first of March 1530. So that they could know what was required of them he also enclosed an outline. The first part was to cover the dogmatical: old and new apostacies from the Catholic faith were to be listed. Then was to follow: changes in the sacraments, adulteration of the scripture, and confusion in the religious life. Finally, the political: Abolishing opposing and vilifying of all spiritual as well as secular governments, riots, bloodshed, disobedience and insolent attack on all divine and human laws.[19]

According to the introduction to the online Concordia transcription of the Eck Theses:

> The Articles begin with the Forty-one Propositions of the Bull of Leo. X. against Luther of Dec. lo, 1520, followed by the Leipzig Theses of Eck against Luther and Carlstadt, and his Eleven Baden Theses against Zwingli and Oecolampadius. Then comes a list of 339 errors ascribed: 203 to Luther, 55 to Zwingli, 48 to Melanchthon, 15 to Bucer, 9 to Oecolampadius, 4 to Bugenhagen, 4 to Osiander. Blaurer, Carlstadt, Pirkheimer, Capito, Rhegias, the Zwickau prophets, the Anabaptists, the Nurnberg preachers, are mingled in one undistinguishable mass, with four "somebodies," acknowledged by Erasmus as his own.[20]

It would seem that Eck wanted to condemn the Lutherans at the Diet before the process had even begun, by prejudging them and not letting the Emperor—as he had requested—*give a charitable hearing to every man's opinion, thoughts, and notions, to understand them, to weigh them, to bring and reconcile them to a unity in Christian truth.* It would seem perhaps that a trap had been laid.

---

19. Reu, *Sources*, 57
20. *Bookofconcord*.eck-404-theses/

# 4

# The Diet of Augsburg 1530

Image of Dr Christian Beyer (1482–1535) addressing the Diet of Augsburg on June 25, 1530. Charles V of the Holy Roman Empire is seated to the left, while Beyer reads the Confession to the Assembly.

On the day of the Assembly, after the Mass, a solemn procession was held to the Council Chamber where the Diet would take place. The Emperor arranged for a thousand foot soldiers to guard all entrances in case of any disturbances occurring. In addition, according to Cochlaeus, he forbade, under serious penalty, that there not be any public sermons at this time, except in the Cathedral Church by the ordinary preacher. The Emperor then gave the floor to the Lutheran princes who had their confession read by Dr. Christian Beyer. Melanchthon's text was read in German, whilst a Latin version was made available for the Emperor. Twenty-one articles were announced, after which a series of abuses were detailed in various other articles. The titles of these were Communion under both kinds, the marriage of priests, the Mass, Confession, Distinction of foods, Monastic vows and ecclesiastical power. What Melanchthon wrote, and at least partially succeeded in doing, was an orthodox 'Catholic' summary of Christian faith and beliefs. He did not intend for it to become the Confession of a newly founded Church, but to correct errors and misconceptions that had been current about the teaching of the Reformers. Therefore, in the 21 Articles Melanchthon sought to correct as many of the false teachings of Eck's 404 theses as possible, by a standard proclamation of Roman Catholic belief. He wished to compose in a non-polemical reasoned manner (with scripture quotations and references from the Church Fathers) the differences between Eck's assertions and the beliefs of the Reformers which he believed represented orthodox Catholic Christianity. While professional theologians might question some details or technicalities of the 21 articles, the general impression given by the Confession to Christian ears is largely unremarkable.

Melanchthon did, however, wish to clarify some specifics from the 404 theses. For example, Articles VII and VIII correct the idea ascribed "to Bucer, Augustine and Wiclif" that "only the predestined are in the church but the wicked or reprobate are not in the church."[1] The CA states to the contrary that "although the church properly is the congregation of saints or true believers, nevertheless, since in this life many hypocrites and evil men are mingled therewith, it is lawful to use the sacraments which are administered by evil men, according to the saying of Christ 'The Scribes and Pharisees sit on Moses seat.' (Matt. 23:2) Both the Sacraments and Word are effective because of Christ's institution and command, even if they are administered by evil men."[2]

1. Reu, *Sources*, 106
2. *The Augsburg Confession*. Article X, 22

This, indeed, is the teaching of the Catechism of the Catholic Church of today: "All members of the Church, including her ministers must acknowledge that they are sinners. In everyone, the weeds of sin will still be mixed with the good wheat of the Gospel until the end of time." Further the Catechism states in accordance with the principal *ex opera operato* "from the moment that a sacrament is celebrated in accordance with the intention of the Church, the power of Christ and his Spirit acts in and through, independently of the personal holiness of the minister."[3]

Article X deals with the Real Presence in the Eucharist to counter Eck's propositions where he 'quotes' Melanchthon and Pirkheimer saying, "In the Eucharist, the substance of bread and wine remains—transubstantiation is a figment of sophists and Romanists."[4]. In the Confession Melanchthon states in Article X, "our churches teach that the body and blood of Christ are truly present and distributed to those who eat the Lord's Supper."[5]

This too is confirmed in the teaching of the Catholic Church in the Catechism: "In the most blessed sacrament of the Eucharist, 'the body and blood, together with the soul and divinity, of our Lord Jesus Christ, and, therefore, the whole Christ is truly, really, and substantially contained.'"[6]

The following longer assertions are made by Eck which doubtless would have affected the Emperor's state of mind. They are given here in full with references as to their origin, as given by Eck:

333 We Christians are free, exempt from all the laws of men, liberated through Baptism (Luther).

334 No laws can be imposed with any right upon Christians, whether by men or by angels, unless so far as they be willing (Luther).

335 Subjects neither can, nor will, nor ought to endure your tyranny any longer (Luther to the Princes).

338 I regret that I submitted to the Emperor at Worms. Whatever tolerance of my doctrine was conceded by my judges is of no account to tyrants (Luther).

339 There is no more excellent secular law than that of the Turk, as he has no canonical and civil law (Luther).

---

3. *Catechism of the Catholic Church*, 219
4. Reu, Sources, /Eck Article No 235
5. *The Augsburg Confession* Article X The Lord's Supper p.23
6. Ratzinger, *The Catechism of the Catholic Church*.346 Par 1374

345 Ever since the beginning of the world, a wise prince has been a most rare bird; for generally they are either the greatest fools or the very worst rascals; for they are God's policemen and executioners (Luther).

366 After one has been justified no laws or ordinances bind him (Melanchthon).

383 There is no hope of a remedy, unless, all the laws of all men being once annulled, we judge and rule all things according to the Gospel (Luther).

384 We must not swear for temporal things; for he who requires an oath of another, or himself swears, must be of a malicious and trifling mind not regarding the truth (Melanchthon).

386 All are heathen who contend in court for property or reputation (Luther)

390 Business contracts even for godly purposes, as churches, benefices, etc. are usurious (Strauss); or at least, unjust (Luther).

391 A community of all things is commanded in the New Testament (Melanchthon).

403 It is proper and in accord with God's word to excite seditions and tumults; hence there is no better proof that my doctrine is of God, than that it excites discords, seditions, and tumults (Luther). Many of them, therefore, have often publicly testified to the common people: "The Gospel wants blood." (Zwingli, etc.)

404 Among Christians, there should be no superiority, no courts, nothing fenced up or closed, no "meum" or "teum," no restraint or excommunication; and this they want to be frequent (Anabaptists)[7]

These assertions—which are attributed truly or falsely to Luther, Melanchthon and also to Zwingli and the Anabaptists—would, if followed, have led to complete anarchy in the Empire. One could suggest they were included to disturb the peace of the Emperor.

## MELANCHTHON'S RESPONSE

The Augsburg Confession Article XVI of Civic Affairs.

---

7. Reu, *Sources*, 100–120

## The Diet of Augsburg 1530

1. Of Civil Affairs they teach that lawful civil ordinances are good works of God, and that...

2. it is right for Christians to bear civil office, to sit as judges, to judge matters by the Imperial and other existing laws, to award just punishments, to engage in just wars, to serve as soldiers, to make legal contracts, to hold property, to make oath when required by the magistrates, to marry a wife, to be given in marriage.

3. They condemn the Anabaptists who forbid these civil offices to Christians.

4. They condemn also those who do not place evangelical perfection in the fear of God and in faith, but in forsaking civil offices,

5. For the Gospel teaches an eternal righteousness of the heart. Meanwhile, it does not destroy the State or the family, but very much requires that they be preserved as ordinances of God, and that charity be practiced in such

6. ordinances. Therefore, Christians are necessarily bound to obey their own magistrates

7. and laws save only when commanded to sin; for then they ought to obey God rather than men. Acts 5:29.[8]

The Catechism of the Catholic Church (1992) again states:

> It is the *duty of citizens* to contribute along with the civil authorities to the good of society in a spirit of truth, justice, solidarity, and freedom. The love and service of *one's country* follow from the duty of gratitude and belong to the order of charity. Submission to legitimate authorities and service of the common good require citizens to fulfill their roles in the life of the political community.[9]

One might question how both Eck's Theses and Melanchthon's Confession might have been examined in a modern Court of Appeal.

- What were Eck's exact references for his attributed statements?
- Were his statements intended to 'poison' and prejudice the audience, and, in this case, the mind of the Emperor?

---

8. Melanchthon Augsburg Confession Article XVI, 27–28.
9. Ratzinger *The Catechism of the Catholic Church*, 540 Par 2239

- Why did he quote from Zwingli and the Anabaptists in the Theses who were not aligned theologically with Luther and the Reformers when the Lutherans were being assessed?
- On the other hand, how might one view Melanchthon's Confession?
- Was he in any way seeking to cover up any excesses in the words or deeds of the Reformers?
- Was he being honest in his stated desire to follow Catholic Church teaching and only to ask questions about abuses?
- Were his sentiments genuinely those of the Reformers or were they being duplicitous and in fact heretical?
- Additionally, one might ask what was actually happening here in the spiritual realm? Jesus said that the unity of the Church would help the world to believe that He was sent from the Father. Was the unity of the Church here being threatened? Was it indeed to be broken by both corruption and scandal?

We can only imagine what was going through the mind of the Emperor as he listened to Gregory Brück (1485–1557)[10] announcing the Confession to the audience having read or acquainted himself with Eck's writing who concluded his 404 theses with the following paragraph:

> All the articles above noted, both those of Luther himself, as clearly a man familiar with the devil, and of those who, being infatuated with his errors, have so degenerated as to become deaf to the truth, we reject and anathematize each of them as heretical, or scandalous, false, and offensive to godly ears, and misleading the simple, or entirely seditious and disturbing the public peace. With respect to this, I am ready to give an account in a public disputation, at the pleasure of the Most Revered Emperor, God aiding me, and the Virgin Mary and all Saints supporting me with their intercessions.'[11]

The 21 Articles of the Confession on the other hand concluded with this irenic statement of Melanchthon:

> This is about the Sum of our Doctrine, in which, as can be seen, there is nothing that varies from the Scriptures, or from the

---

10. Legal Advisor to Martin Luther and called 'the Lawyer of the Reformation. He represented the Protestant faith at the creation of the Schmalkaldic league in 1532.

11. Reu, Sources,120

Church Catholic, or from the Church of Rome as known from its writers. This being the case, they judge harshly who insist that our teachers be regarded as heretics. There is, however, disagreement on certain abuses, which have crept into the Church without rightful authority. And even in these, if there were some difference, there should be proper lenity on the part of bishops to bear with us by reason of the Confession which we have now reviewed; because even the Canons are not so severe as to demand the same rites everywhere, neither, at any time, have the rites of all churches been the same; although, among us, in large part, the ancient rites are diligently observed. For it is a false and malicious charge that all the ceremonies, all the things instituted of old, are abolished in our churches. But it has been a common complaint that some abuses were connected with the ordinary rites. These, inasmuch as they could not be approved with a good conscience, have been to some extent corrected.'[12]

The complete 28 Articles of the Augsburg Confession are readily available on line and in the published editions of Concordia Publishing[13]. Both at the time, and many times between 1530 and the present, they have been examined by a wide range of scholars and theologians. They are currently (2025) being re-examined by a group of Catholic and Lutheran Theologians at the request of the Lutheran World Federation, the International Lutheran Council and the Pontifical Dicastery for the Promotion of Christian Unity. We will examine some of the questions that they are facing in this joint review later in this volume.[14]

12. https://bookofconcord.org/augsburg-confession/

13. The Augsburg Confession https://www.gutenberg.org/files/275/275-h/275-h.htm

14. On March 1, 2024, the Dicastery for Promoting Christian Unity (DPCU) hosted the inaugural meeting of the Concordia Lutheran–Catholic Augustana Working Group, which met in Rome until March 2, 2024.

Cardinal Kurt Koch, Prefect of the DPCU, welcomed the members of the working group and encouraged them to explore the pre-confessional/ecumenical potential of the Augsburg Confession in more detail in view of the 500th anniversary of the *Confessio Augustana* in 2030. And https://thebookofconcord.org/augsburg-confession/

The Augustana Working Group includes representatives of the International Lutheran Council and the Catholic Church. Following the conclusion of the theological conversations between the International Lutheran Council, an association of Concordia Lutheran churches, and the Catholic Church (2014–2019), both sides suggested the establishment of a working group as a distinct ecumenical-theological format.

The working group is not an official dialogue commission. The aim is not to produce a document of churchly consensus. However, the publication of the results of the joint research is intended to enrich the ecumenical discussion in an indirect way. http://www.

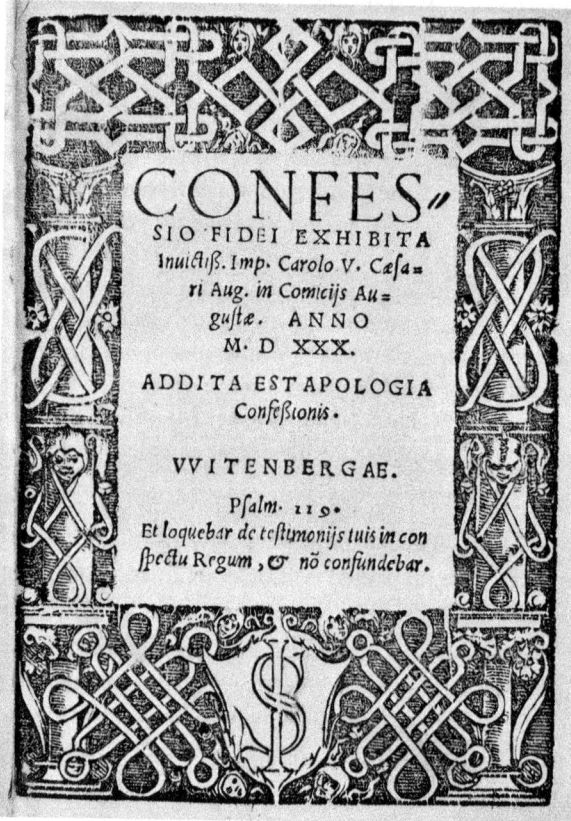

Early printing in Latin of the Augsburg Confession made in Wittenberg in 1535.

# 5

# The Confutation

How in fact did the Emperor react to the hearing of the Confession?

According to Cochlaeus, the Emperor had patiently listened to the Reformers until the end and accepted a copy of the Confession. As it was now late, the company was dismissed but not before ordering that the theologians of the Catholic princes prepare a refutation of the Confession. The Papal Legate gave strict instructions on how to go about this task: each article was to be examined to see if it was suspicious in any way or obscure, and, if so, for its meaning to be made clear "in all humility shrewdness, politeness and Christian love." What was acceptable was to be laudably accepted, and all sections which deviated from pure Christian faith were to be destroyed. In this case, it had to be shown that such an idea or belief was heretical and had previously been condemned as such. If the Protestant Princes objected that errors had been wrongly attributed to them, they were instructed to refer them to statements made previously by the Reformers, and to show how they were different from the Confession. These heretical statements then should be contrasted with positive statements from the Catholic Church. All of this was then to be given to the Emperor in both Latin and German, where it would be discussed with the Catholic princes and then read out to the convened Diet. It then had to be either accepted or rejected by the Lutherans, whilst no third alternative or compromise was to be admitted. In closing the Legate reminded the Emperor of the conquering and defeat of the Saxons by Charlemagne and thus the possible use of force against the Evangelicals.[1]

According to the Concordia version, the theologians—who included both Eck and Cochlaeus, (both of whom were very antagonistic to Luther) spent several days preparing a lengthy response of 280 pages, which included assertions to prove that Luther and the Reformers had long taught, which were erroneous and had been corrected in the Confession. In the original draft of the *Confutation,* an aggressive stance was immediately adopted with threats and proposals to destroy all the books and pamphlets of the Reformers. The second article of the unpublished first draft of the Confutation states:

> 'There appear in the aforenamed confession certain articles through which, incessantly, during the last ten years conflicting and contrary things have been publicly disseminated and divulged among the inexperienced multitude by the preachers in many pamphlets and sermons, which fact is made manifest by the books that they have broadcast far and wide. In order that these things no longer cause the wretched common people to vacillate in doubt and to be involved in inextricable errors, the best thing to do would seem to be that pamphlets and books of that kind would be destroyed and abolished by an imperial edict, especially also since the preachers have of their own accord renounced their errors here and in part at a visitation in Saxony'.[2]

The fifth article suggested:

> although the princes themselves and the preachers detest these heresies and hostile sects, and do not in the least approve of them, yet it is apparent that the fountainhead and origin of them all is Luther and his wicked, frivolous, and self-contradictory doctrine. Therefore it seems advisable for Your Imperial Majesty to direct your eyes and your mind to distinguishing these things to the glory of the Highest God and the tranquility of the Roman Empire and its subjects, and to weed out by their deepest roots and to extirpate radically and as fast as possible such abominable heresies of unheard-of wickedness, and the discords, and inner wars and tumults, and to see to it that neither the princes nor the two cities in their provinces and places tolerate these sects and their instigators

---

1. Reu, *Sources,*116
2. Reu, Sources,327.

## The Confutation

nor allow new ones to crop up, but that they hasten to embrace again the old Catholic religion.[3]

One of the group, Compegius, tried to connect the teaching of the Anabaptists to the influence of Luther, saying that they were guilty of unchastity and that they denied both the divinity of Jesus and that Mary was the Mother of God. According to Reu,

> they could not be satisfied with a simple confutation of Lutheran doctrine. They expected to present a mass of documents which would ruthlessly open the Emperor's eyes to Luther and his activities, which were not apparent from their Confession. So, from the material at hand, they gathered passages which were to show Luther's heresies, proving that they were merely revivals of discarded heresies, and that he continually contradicted himself. Fabri says: 'One book contradicts the other, one statement, one word, yes even one letter the other, in a word, Luther has become a mad irrational being.[4]

To conclude, the writers of the *Confutato* urged the Emperor not to heed the call of the Reformers for a Christian council, since it would fail to quieten the voices of dissent and would demonstrate to the whole Church the poor example of German Church life. The Emperor, however, was well informed about the abuses in Germany and, refusing the advice of the Legate, wrote a letter to the Pope demanding a free and open Christian Council.[5] The Princes also wished to create peace and concord and as the Emperor had required, were asked to shorten the Confutation and only relate to the Articles of the Confession. The initial document was read in the sessions of the Catholic estates, taking nine to ten hours. Only a few accepted it because of its harsh tone, and the document was rejected by the majority. The document had to be completely revised, keeping only that which was in harmony with the Scriptures and "all that was malicious, sullen and unnecessary" to be removed. Eck returned to the task, realizing he had to renounce all the negative passages that they had given in great detail, and to stick to the points requested by the Emperor.

After five attempts and six weeks of preparation, the Emperor finally agreed to accept the text. It was now 12 pages long and had largely been

---

3. Reu, *Sources*, 328–29.
4. Reu, *Sources*, 120
5. Reu, *Sources*, 122

refined and redrafted, omitting most negativity and rancor.[6] Finally on August 3, 1530, the Confutation was ready and read to the Emperor by Alexander Schweiss, who was his private secretary. The Emperor was content that the Confession agreed with Catholic teaching on many points and that the Lutherans rejected all the abuses that had marred the Church in Germany. Cochlaeus relates that many of the Lutherans "laughed inappropriately" during the reading, while others were noting down the passages and scriptures read, so that they, in turn, could confute the Confutation.[7] When the refutation was complete, the Catholic princes present signaled their approval of the text, and the Lutheran princes were asked by them to accept and approve the confutation. The Lutheran princes, however, asked for a copy of the Confutation, but the Emperor refused. Both Cochlaeus and the Concordia account state reasons for the refusal. Concordia states they were given on condition that they would not reply in writing, that they did not publicize the Confutation, or print it, and that they would join the Emperor and the Catholic Estates in "concurring with the Confutation on every point".[8] The Lutherans would not accept these demands. During this time Melanchthon had heard that the Papal Legate was willing to accept Communion under both kinds and to accept the marriage of priests. In what Reu describes as a "moment of weakness" Melanchthon wrote a letter to the Legate, saying:

> We have no dogma which is diverse from that of the Roman Church; we have also rebuked many who dared to spread dangerous dogmas for which public testimony is available. We are ready to obey the Roman Church if they, with the same charitableness which they have always shown to all people, either ignore or drop certain few things which we, even if we would, could not change. We venerate the authority of the Roman Pope and the whole church government, if only the Roman Pontifex, does not cast us aside. But if harmony is so easily reestablished if your clemency yields in a few things and we obey in good faith then why should it be necessary to reject those who plead or to persecute them with fire and sword? For no other reason do we endure so much hatred in Germany than that we defend the dogmas of the Roman Church with so much firmness. We shall in future, until

---

6. Reu, *Sources* 124–25 The Latin text of the Confutado was published in 1573 while the German version was only printed in 1808.

7. Vandiver, *Two lives*, 251

8. Reu, *Sources*, 127 Vandiver, *Two lives*, 251

## The Confutation

our end, also remain true to Christ and the Roman Church even if you should refuse to mercifully receive us.[9]

There was still a degree of good will to see if matters could be resolved peaceably. The Emperor was perturbed that agreement had not been reached and that the Lutherans would not accept the conditions he had given. The Catholic princes also felt that further efforts should be made in the impasse. The Emperor thus agreed to have a delegation of 17 members to resolve the issue: both sides were asked to come for a discussion at the Chapter House of the Greater Church of Augsburg on Sunday 7th August. The Marquis of Brandenburg began the proceedings encouraging the re-establishment of faith with the rest of the Empire, fearing that, if this were not to happen, then there would be (as Cochlaeus relates) "wars, uprisings, and devastations of the provinces."[10] Dr. Gregory Bruck spoke declaring that they were upset by the threats that had been given by the Diet. They also felt that they had not been sufficiently heard by the Emperor and that a copy of the Confutation had not been given to them "without oppressive conditions". They also felt that they could not agree to a Confutation which they were not freely able to examine. Finally, they noted that a promise had been made previously to hold a Church Council, but nothing had since happened. The princes responded that, if the Diet failed to produce an agreement "a great number of the common folk would again be incited to rebellion."[11] They added that the reason that they were not given the Confutation was because the Edict of Worms had been "publicly and openly derided, despised and perverted by their preachers' actions which showed dishonor, contempt and mockery both toward His Imperial Majesty and toward all the other princes and estates of the Empire." For this reason, it had been held back. In addition, the Lutherans were reminded that public dispute regarding matters of faith was punishable by law, under the penalty of death, and that they "should really fear withdrawing from the Communion of the Church and to trust more in Apostates than in the Roman Church, the Holy Fathers and the general Councils," contributing to the "destruction of many." Finally, they excused the Emperor from calling a Church Council, as he was at war with both France and the Turks, and that Luther had considered the Council of Worms "of no account."[12] For all

9. Reu, *Sources* 127
10. Vandiver *Two lives*. 251
11. Vandiver, *Two lives*, 252
12. Vandiver, *Two Lives*, .252–53

these reasons, the Lutherans were asked to reconsider their position and to return to the Church rather than leaving it in schism. According to the account made by Cochlaeus the Lutherans took these conclusions badly and asked for a period of time to deliberate among themselves.

After some deliberation, they requested that nothing that others had written about them should be imputed to them, and they further suggested that a smaller, equal number of Catholics and Lutherans be selected ,- ones who understood the gravity of the situation—and were also 'inclined to peace and agreement'. To this end two groups were established, including Cochlaeus and Johannes Eck with Melanchthon and three Lutheran theologians, none of whom had Doctoral degrees in Theology.[13]

---

13. Vandiver, *Two Lives* .254

# 6

# Fateful Days

ON THE 15TH OF August the group gathered in the anteroom of the Council Chamber. After simple preliminaries, the Confession was once again put forward to be examined. one article at a time. The time was fruitful and more hopeful and by the late evening the group had managed to agree on the wording of eleven of the articles. The following day, they continued to make progress and were able to agree on 15 of the 21 Articles. They still had disagreements over three and these were relegated to the final part of the Confession. The articles which caused most difficulties were the final seven articles. These listed the abuses experienced by the evangelicals, which had prompted the whole Diet in the first place. On the 22nd August the Catholics reported their achievements to the Princes, and everything seemed to be heading towards agreement from both sides. In his description of this stage Cochlaeus was partisan, calling the Evangelicals "stubborn." However, they continued their work, now using a smaller group of six, still including Luther's protagonist Johannes Elk.

Luther entered the whole discussion, as it were, 'through a back door'. Though not present, his words and works were being spread abroad to the public. His letter to the Archbishop and Cardinal of Mainz was published and made available in Augsburg. In it, in his own typical Lutheran fashion, he berated all including the Pope and the Emperor. He then went further, by writing a short book dedicated to all the Princes of the Church in Augsburg called *Admonition to the Churchmen at Augsburg assembled in the Imperial*

*Diet.* This book became freely available in Augsburg for all to read—including the Princes and theologians. It was full of Luther's undiplomatic rhetoric and thunder, a diatribe excoriating all for the abuses that had been experienced during this time in Germany, calling—in a voice like an old Testament prophet—the whole Church to repentance for so much evil and distortion of the Gospel. He wrote:

> The reason is that my conscience drives me to pray, beseech and exhort each and all of you, in the kindliest way and from the heart, that you will not pass this diet by or use it to vain purposes. For God, through our most gracious Emperor Charles, is giving you grace, chance, time, and cause to accomplish much that is great and good by means of this diet, if only you have the will to do so. He is speaking now as Paul speaks in Corinthians 6:1, "I exhort you that ye receive not the gift of God in vain.". . .If, however, this diet shall break up without result (which may God graciously forbid!) and nothing worthwhile be accomplished, after all the world has for a long while been fed with false hopes and put off by diets and councils, and that hope has all been false and vain, it is to be feared that despair will be bred, and everyone will become overtired of false hopes and delays, and the long, fruitless waiting will produce impatience and make bad blood. For things cannot longer stay as they now are, especially with you and your class; you know and feel that better than I can tell you. I am therefore doing what now I do, for your own good and for the sake of peace and unity.[1]

It was as if Luther's towering voice could be heard lurking in the background, while the discussions were in session at the Council Chamber. Cochlaeus,—probably thus emboldened by Luther's rhetoric,—brought forth an older passage of Luther's challenging writings. Eck then decided to add another challenging quote, seemingly wanting to embarrass the milder spoken Melanchthon—who he said 'blushed' hearing Luther's penetrating words, and then admitted that Luther had indeed written them:

"When did he write these things? "asked Duke Frederick.

"Perhaps ten years ago," replied Melanchthon.

The Catholics then responded :

---

1. "Exhortation to clergy at Augsburg" Book of Concord Martin Luther Accessed 12/5/2023 https://bookofconcord.org/other-resources/sources-and-context/luthers-exhortation-clergy-augsburg/

"What does that matter. It is enough for us that this is the opinion of the very man himself !.²"

Two others from the Evangelicals then retorted that they were not there to debate Luther's writings, but to defend their Confession of faith and asked for Luther's writings to be left aside.

As previously during the colloquium, some articles of the Lutherans had been approved while others were not; the Electors and Princes wished to make a detailed study of the Confutation to check more closely the articles that were attributed to them were quoted correctly. As the Emperor promised to hear both sides, they once again requested that a copy of the Confutation be released for their inspection.[3] The Emperor had said that he would deal kindly with the Lutherans, and on August 4th he finally granted their request, but on certain conditions. He stipulated that the Lutherans "must come to an agreement with the Catholic princes and estates; furthermore that they spare His Imperial Majesty with their refutations and make no further reply and, above all, that they keep this and other writings to themselves, nor let them pass out of their hands, for instance, by printing them or in any other way."[4] The Lutherans agreed to this condition, "as far as it was possible to do so with God and their conscience". When, however, they were warned that should there ever be a leak of the document, the Emperor would no longer confer with them, they decided to decline the offer. They added that they would still answer the Confutation, as they had noted the most important parts while it was read aloud during the Diet.

The arguments then continued for a period without any more progress until they were adjourned with a request that, before April 15th the following year, the Evangelicals should give a "sealed response on the question of all matters whether they wished to agree in faith with His Imperial Majesty and the other Estates of the Empire or not." They were then instructed that nothing new on the question of faith should be published or sold in their lands. In addition, they were ordered that anyone who remained Catholic in their lands "should not be driven into their own sect." The Emperor concluded by urging the Electors of the Augsburg Confession to remain in the "ancient religion of their ancestors."[5]

2. Vandiver *Two lives*, 256
3. Bente *Historical Introductions* Article 50
4. Bente *Historical Introductions* Article 50
5. Vandiver *Two Lives*,.258

## Una Sancta

The Diet concluded without resolution on November 19th. In the meantime, the Augsburg Confession was published in Augsburg and Cochlaeus sought to have the Confutation printed without success. He summarized by saying, "for this reason it happened that to this very day, though certainly not unworthy of the light, it has not been published."[6] The Introduction to the Confutation on the Concordia website gives a different inflection saying, "all subsequent pleading and imploring however on the part of Eck and the others to induce the Emperor to publish the Confutation fell on deaf ears." They surmise that Charles no longer took any interest in a "document that had so shamefully shattered his fond ambition of reconciling the religious parties."[7] Concordia further says that the refusal to print the Confutation was "an admission on the part of the Romanists of a guilty conscience and of being ashamed themselves of the Document."[8] Luther himself commented on the lack of publication:

> If it is so precious a thing and so well founded in the Scriptures as they bellow and boast, why, then, does it shun the light? What benefit can there be in hiding from us and everyone else such public matters as must nevertheless be taught and held among them? But if it is unfounded and futile, why, then, did they in the first resolution [of the Diet], have the Elector of Brandenburg proclaim and publish in writing that our Confession had been refuted [by the Confutation] with the Scriptures and stanch arguments? If that were true, and if their own consciences did not give them the lie, they would not merely have allowed such precious and well-founded Refutation to be read, but would have furnished us with a written copy, saying:
>
> There you have it; we defy anyone to answer it! . . . as we did and still do with our Confession . . . For this well-founded refutation [Confutation] has as yet not come to light but is perhaps sleeping with the old Tannhauser on Mount Venus.[9]

---

6. Vandiver *Two Lives*, 258
7. Bente *historical-introductions*, Article 45
8. Bente *Historical Introductions* Article 45
9. Bente *Historical Introductions* Article 47 The Confutation was only published in Latin over forty years later in 1573 and nearly 300 years later in German in 1808.

## MELANCHTHON'S APOLOGY

During the reading of the Confutation Melanchthon was already considering writing an Apology for the Confession. However, it was only on August 29th that official action was taken to prepare an Apology for the Lutheran position, an effective answer to the claims of the Confutation. When the matter was discussed the delegates of Nuremberg declared that "in case His Majesty refused to deliver to us the Confutation of our Confession without restrictions [the aforementioned conditions] we nevertheless could not refrain from writing a reply to it, as far as the articles had been noted down during the reading, and from delivering it to His Imperial Majesty: we therefore ought to prepare ourselves in this matter, in order to make use of it in case of necessity."[10] Whereupon the Saxons were commissioned to prepare an Apology and they chose Melanchthon to draft the Document. In his Preface he states, "They had, however, commanded me and some others to prepare an Apology of the Confession, in which the reasons why we could not accept the Confutation should be set forth to His Imperial Majesty, and the objections made by the adversaries be refuted."[11] By September 20th Melanchthon had finished his draft. He wrote

> I have in these days written the Apology of our Confession, which, if necessary, shall also be delivered; for it will be opposed to the Confutation of the other party, which you heard when it was read. I have written it sharply and more vehemently" (than the Confession).[12]

An opportunity came for it to be presented when again the Imperial decision was repeated, saying that the Confession had been refuted by the Confutation. The Verdict was declared that "the Emperor in the presence of the other electors, princes, and estates of the holy empire, graciously heard the opinion and confession [of the Evangelical princes], had given it due and thorough consideration, and had refuted and disproved it with sound arguments from the holy gospels and the Scriptures."[13] This declaration opened the door to present a copy of Melanchthon's Apology. In the name of the Elector, Brueck re-iterated that the Lutherans were only offered a copy under impossible conditions, but nevertheless, on the basis of what they had heard they could now offer a 'counter-plea'. He then asked if he

10. Bente Historical Introductions, Article 52
11. Bente *Historical Introductions* Article 52
12. Bente *Historical Introductions*, Article 53
13. Bente *Historical Introductions*, Article 53

could present it, as it gave "strong irrefutable reasons from Holy Scripture to underscore the integrity of the Confession." The Duke initially took the Apology, but, upon a signal from the Emperor, returned it,—unread.

Relations between the Emperor and the Catholic Princes with the Lutherans were thus severed and indeed this was to become permanent. On September 23rd, the Elector left Augsburg and by the 19th of November, all the Evangelical Princes had left. A second edict was issued by the Papal theologians. In it the Emperor "sanctioned all dogmas and abuses which the Evangelicals had attacked, confirmed the spiritual jurisdiction of the bishops, demanded the restoration of all abolished rites, identified himself with the Confutation, and repeated the assertion that the Lutheran Confession had been refuted from the Scriptures."[14]

The whole experience had a deep effect on the normally mild mannered and cautious Melanchthon. Immediately afterwards, Melanchthon set about recasting the Apology which was finally published 47 years after the Diet had concluded. While doing this he drew out further references for the position of the evangelicals; he also showed his deep concern, and one could say even filial devotion to the church. What was happening to the Church disturbed him; he had no peace in the division he could see occurring. Timothy Wengert, Professor Emeritus of Reformation History at the Lutheran Theological Seminary at Philadelphia, in an essay called *Phillip Melanchthon's last word to Cardinal Lorenzo Campeggio*, describes how Melanchthon showed his deep frustration at the failure to agree at Augsburg, witnessing the break-up of Western Christianity.[15] In the middle of Article XII of the Apology on "Confession and Satisfaction", Melanchthon takes a digression which was highly charged and out of his normal unassuming character: he decides to publicly rebuke Cardinal Campeggio by name, blaming him for the collapse of the discussions. He becomes incensed with the poor attempt to use scripture against the Augsburg Confession, and then turns his anger on the Pope himself for assigning such poor and incompetent people to judge the Confessions of the Lutherans. Wengert suggests that this is a shot aimed directly at Eck, Cochlaeus and Fabri. He states that the job should have been given to 'judges of great learning and personal faith instead'. Melanchthon then sets his aim upon the Cardinal:

---

14. Bente *Historical Introductions* Article 53

15. Wengert Timothy j. Essay 4 *Phillip Melanchthon's Last Word to Cardinal Lorenzo Campeggio* https://www.vr-elibrary.de/doi/abs/10.13109/9783666550478

Painting of Phillip Melanchthon 1497–1560—Author of Augsburg Confession and Apology by Lucas Cranach the Elder (1532).

Since we include almost all of the Christian doctrine in the Confession, judges should have been appointed to declare about important and various matters. Their learning and faith would have been more acceptable than the learning of these philosophers who have written this Confutation. It was very fitting of you, O Campegius, according to your wisdom, to have made sure that they should write nothing about important matters that, either now or later, might appear to lower respect for the Roman See. If the Roman See determines that all nations should recognize her as mistress of the faith, she should try very hard to have educated and godly people investigate religious matters. What will the world conclude if at any time the adversaries' writing is brought to light? What will future generations think about these disgraceful judicial

# UNA SANCTA

investigations? You see, O Campegius, that these are the last days. Christ predicted that the great greatest danger to religion would happen in them (Matthew 24:9-28). You, who should sit on the watchtower (Hosea 9:8) and control religious matters, should in these times also use unusual wisdom and diligence. Unless you heed them, there are many signs that threat- make a mistake if you think that churches should be kept only by force and arms. The people are asking to be taught about religion. How many do you suppose there are, not only in Germany, but also in England, in Spain, in France, in Italy, and finally even in the city of Rome? Since controversies have come up about subjects of the greatest importance, they are beginning to doubt here and there, to be silently insulted that you refuse to investigate and rightly judge such weighty subjects. They doubt and are insulted that you do not help wavering consciences, that you only ask us to be overthrown and destroyed by arms. To many good people this doubt is more bitter than death".[16]

This was, in reality, a 'true son of the Church' rebuking his father—demonstrating the broken heart of a reformer, and not the ire of a revolutionary who wished to overthrow the religious establishment. Wengert says, it was for such reasons that during the 500th anniversary of his birth, Melanchthon was called "The Father of Ecumenism.".[17] To Wengert, in handing over the task to partisans instead of giving it to erudite prayerful scholars, the Cardinal undermined the very thing that he wished to uphold: the teaching authority of the church itself. By being complicit in a possible attack on the Lutheran princes, the Cardinal left the church open to disdain and ridicule. Showing real concern for the flocks of the church, Melanchthon requested proper instruction in matters of faith and religion and felt that the church had not only undermined its own reputation, but had "missed the signs of the times, ignoring concerns of sensitive, thinking people and had trivialized the matter."

Melanchthon's Apology became, with the Augsburg Confession, one of the essential Documents of the Lutheran Church, which looks to Augsburg and 1530 as its foundation.

Recalling these events the following year, Luther remarked:

---

16. Concordia *The Lutheran Confessions* Concordia The Apology of Melanchthon Article XII Confession and Satisfaction .201

17. Wengert *Phillip Melanchthon's Last Words* 1

if they had not felt that their boasting was lying, pure and simple, they would not only gladly, and without offering any objections, have surrendered their refutation as was so earnestly desired, but would also have made use of all printing-presses to publish it, and heralded it with all trumpets and drums, so that such defiance would have arisen that the very sun would not have been able to shine on account of it. But now, since they so shamefully withheld their answer and still more shamefully hide and secrete it, by this action their evil conscience bears witness to the fact that they lie like reprobates when they boast that our Confession has been refuted, and that by such lies they seek not the truth, but our dishonor and a cover for their shame.'[18]

The Apology for the Augsburg Confession is included with the Confession in summary of Lutheran beliefs called *The Book of Concord*. This was initially published in Dresden, Saxony in 1580. More recently the *Book of Concord* itself was revised, updated and annotated with both documents in the modern edition of the Lutheran Confessions called *Concordia*.[19] The two documents marked the beginnings of the Lutheran Church, now a 'denomination', separate from the Roman Catholic Church

---

18. Bente *Historical Introductions* Article 53
19. Dau and Bente 'Concordia' The Lutheran Confessions A Readers Edition of the Book of Concord Concordia Publishing House St Louis 2005.

# 7

# The Confession Spreads

### THE BREAK UP OF EUROPE

JOHANN MICHAEL REU FIRST gathered, in English translation, all the information about the writing of the Augsburg Confession, in his book of 1930, *The Augsburg Confession: A Collection of sources*. According to Reu, in spite of attempt by the Emperor to dissuade them, the Confession was soon adapted by others as a Confession and Doctrinal Basis for Christian faith. In 1530, Duke Albrecht of Prussia decreed that "if anyone shall teach anything contrary to the Augsburg Confession, he shall be excommunicated, and if he does not recant, he shall be cast out from the Church absolutely."[1] On February 27th, 1531, the Schmalkaldic League was founded and then perfected in Schweinfurt with the Augsburg Confession as the Confession of the League. In 1532 the Augsburg Confession became authoritative in the Leagues of "Saxony, Hesse, Braunschweig-Lueneburg, Braunschweig-Grubenhagen, Anhalt-Köthen (Prince Wolfgang), Mansfeld and in the cities of Strassburg, Ulm, Konstanz, Reutlingen, Memmingen, Lindau, Biberach, Isny Lübeck, Magdeburg and Bremen." Other territories (not members of the League) also adopted the Confession, including Mark Brandenburg and the city of Nuernberg.[2] All members who subsequently

---

1. Reu *Sources*, 142
2. Reu, *Sources*, 142

joined had to pledge to "have the Word of God and the Pure Doctrine of the Confession uniformly taught and preached."[3] .The Saxon Articles of Visitation of 1533 directed that Churches have in hand both the German and Latin version of the Confession, in order that new ministers should be able to study them and teach them.

From all this activity—at least at this stage—there was no sense that a 'new independent Church' had actually been formed. The Confession was viewed as a part of the 'whole church', and indeed, in anticipation of the (Trent) Council, the theologians were required to review again the Confession and the Apology and to "strengthen it with new arguments from the Scripture and the Fathers." They added that "no changes were to be made to the Confession, only that the nature of the Papacy would be defined more clearly."[4] The Reformers still certainly considered themselves as part of the Roman Catholic church. In 1533, Phillip Melanchthon wrote statutes for the Faculty of Theology at the University of Wittenberg. The opening article stated:

> As in the churches of our dominion and in the juvenile schools, so in the University, in which there ought always to be clear supervision and oversight in doctrine, we will that the pure doctrine of the Gospel be piously and faithfully set forth, preserved and promulgated in harmony with the Confession we delivered to the Emperor Charles at Augsburg in the year 1530, which doctrine we firmly believe to be the pure and uninterrupted consensus of the *Catholic Church of God.*[5]

In Wittenberg, as in other places which adopted the Confession, there is not any notion that this activity is in any sense schismatic, pointing towards a separate denomination; rather the events at Augsburg were viewed as an attempt of Church reform, whilst awaiting the confirmation by a Church Council and ultimately by the universal Catholic Church. Because of this, the Reformers were rigorous in making sure that candidates for Orders and those who took degrees at the Faculty at Wittenberg had to pledge an oath to the Augsburg Confession. In fact, after 1535 no one was allowed to train for the ministry who was not in agreement with the Articles of the Confession. Before ordination, new ministers had to face an examination which included a pledge to teach and preach "in harmony

---

3. Reu, *Sources*, 143
4. Reu, *Sources*, 143
5. Reu, *Sources*, 144 (authors italics added for emphasis)

with the Lutheran doctrines expressed in the examination papers." During the years of 1537–1555, over 1700 pastors were ordained at Wittenberg all in support of the Confession.

In 1551, the Lutherans found it necessary to prepare for participation in the Council of Trent, and asked Melanchthon, in the northern part of Germany, and Brenz, in the southern part, to work on Confessions. Those supplements to the Augsburg Confession were known as the *Confessio Saxonica* and The *Confession Wuertemberica*. In the first paragraph of the preface to the *Confessio Saxonica*, it is declared:

> We mean simply and faithfully to reiterate the sum of the doctrine which is preached in all the churches that embrace the Confession of the Reverend Dr. Luther, and we repeat the doctrine of the Confession which was presented to the Emperor Charles at the Diet of Augsburg in the year 1530, although some things are here more fully recited. This Repetition was endorsed and approved by synods, universities, superintendents and theologians from Prussia to Strassburg "[6]

## THE PEACE OF AUGSBURG 1555

On September 25, 1555, a measure of peace was brought between the different factions of what was called 'The Peace of Augsburg'. From this time, the German Empire would guarantee religious freedom to all who accepted the Augsburg Confession. According to Reu, the Lutherans:

> wrung from the Catholics the Decree of absolute religious independence in the sense and to the extent that neither the Emperor, nor the King of the Romans, nor any Prince or Estate of the Empire, for any cause or pretext whatever, shall attack or injure the adherents of the Augsburg Confession on account of their religious faith; nor shall they by command, nor in any other way, force any adherent of the Augsburg Confession to forsake his religion, or to abandon the ceremonies already instituted or hereafter to be instituted; and the Emperor and the King and the Estates shall suffer them without hindrance to profess the religion of the Augsburg Confession, and peacefully to enjoy their goods, possessions, rents and rights.[7]

6. Reu *Sources*, 146

7. Reu *Sources*, 147 It is of note that the two original versions of the Confession in Latin and German which were presented to the Emperor in 1530 have been lost and were

# The Confession Spreads

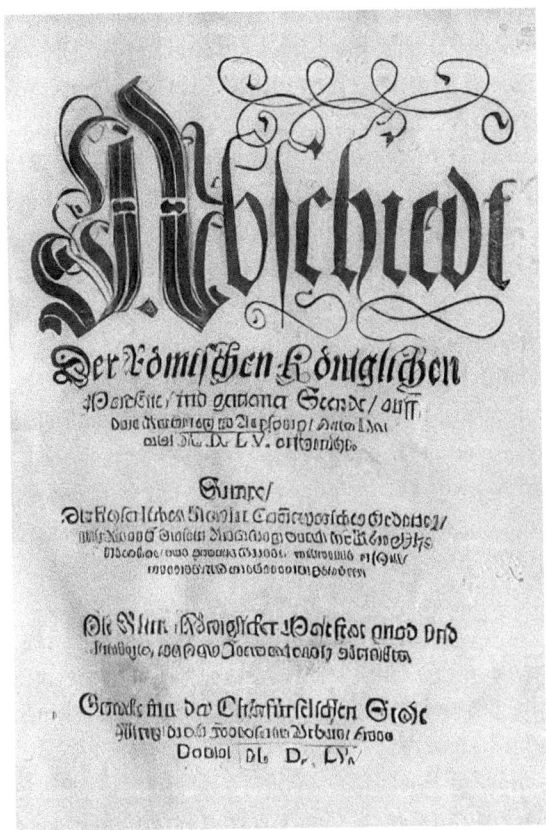

The Peace of Augsburg was signed in 1555, giving equal rights to Lutherans and Catholics. The 'peace' was broken later by the Edict of Restitution of 1629 which restored Catholic ownership of land, leading to the Catholic-Lutheran Thirty Years War.

Despite the rejection at Augsburg, the Reformers had not given up in their quest for complete Church reformation. It is interesting to note that as late as the 1950's, a group of German Lutheran Pastors and theologians called *Die Sammlung* (meaning 'the Gathering') wrote a book called *The Unfinished Reformation*. This book regarded the work of Augsburg

---

(up to at least 1930)—never located. Whilst many copies of the text were duplicated and then circulated across Germany an exact wording of the original Confession is hard to find. In his time Melanchthon was aware of this and immediately following his time in Augsburg began to write an official version of the Confession. Even up to 1930 and the publication of Reu's Book, an original Latin text was awaited to help to create the most accurate version of the Confession.

as unfinished, not having achieved its goal of Church Reform.[8] In many ways, the Reformation was more like a renewal movement of its time which had rediscovered the heart of the Gospel and thus wanted to see the whole Church captured by genuine religious revival and personal faith in Jesus as Savior and Messiah. One might perhaps compare it with the renewal movement of the 1960's in the Catholic Church at Vatican 2 when Pope Saint John XXIII had called for a "new Pentecost". A movement blossomed which was initially called *Catholic Pentecostalism*. Later it became better known as the *Catholic Charismatic Renewal*. It was itself not born from the heart of the Church or by any liturgical reform or catechetical directive for adult faith development, but from the periphery. It grew, in fact, from a movement in America which itself was very ecumenical and deeply influenced by Pentecostal groups and fellowships. Though subsequently there were groups within 'the Renewal' who left mainstream Catholicism for Pentecostal Churches and fellowships, most of the renewal groups and fellowships in different countries sought to find themselves in the heart of the Church, seeking recognition from it, its hierarchy and finally from the Papal Office itself. One could suggest that, unlike the 'Renewal movement' of the Reformation, the 'Charismatic renewal' *did* succeed in winning the favor of all the current Popes since the Council, from Paul VI to Pope Francis. The 'Lutheran/Augsburg evangelical movement' did not get such recognition—at least- not yet!

The failure of the reconciliation had deep political repercussions which today in a more pluralistic world, would not have been problematic. The Empire itself was a Catholic 'Holy Roman Empire', and when peace was established between the two groups in the Church in 1555 at the Peace of Augsburg, it also had political effects. By the declaration of *Cuius Regio, eius Regio* (whose realm, whose religion), the princes of the different German states could choose whatever stream of Christianity they wanted,—the traditional faith or the faith of the Augsburg Confession. Only that faith (with a few exceptions) would be allowed in each territory. According to the 'Peace', inhabitants who were not able to conform to either religion, –Catholicism or Lutheranism,—were free to leave or in some cases forced to choose between conversion or migration. Reu says "Those who refused were to be treated according to the terms of the *'beneficium emigrandi'*, the confessors of the Augsburg Confession were permitted to emigrate, with

---

8. Asmussen, Hans et al *The Unfinished Reformation: Katholische Reformation'* 1958 Schwabenverlag Stuttgart

## The Confession Spreads

wife and children to some other country and sell their property after making just payment for release from their vassalage and other taxes."[9] This also applied to the Catholic community, so thus the German states were divided politically and religiously, with the Lutheran states in the north and the Catholic states mostly in the South. Chances now of religious dialog were greatly diminished, as both the words 'Catholicism' and 'Lutheranism' (or 'Evangelicalism') had political connotations.[10] The split was not confined to Germany; now all of Europe was starting to split. Groups of those sympathetic to Luther and the Augsburg Confession started to appear in Bohemia, Moravia, Silesia and Hungary, while translations of the Confession appeared in the Czech lands. The influence of Lutheranism was strongly felt in the Scandinavian Countries. King Christian III, who reigned in Denmark from 1536–1558, brought the Reformation to Denmark. He knew Martin Luther personally, and in 1536 declared that Denmark should become Lutheran. The new faith was then passed on to Norway, where Lutheranism became the official state church in 1539. In 1550, Lutheranism became the official State Church of Iceland. Sweden became a Lutheran state in 1593, as did Finland in the same year. There were also major Lutheran churches in Estonia and Latvia. The Augsburg Confession was also key in the development of Anglicanism. In 1534, just four years after the Augsburg Diet, the Church of England declared its independence from Rome. While some factions in the English church only wanted to keep the traditional faith without the leadership of Rome, another faction, led by Cranmer, the Archbishop of Canterbury, wanted to see real reform throughout the Anglican community, rooting out abuses and outdated customs. Thomas Cromwell, as Lord Privy Seal to Henry VIII, had an English version of the Augsburg Confession, which was printed in 1536 with Royal permission. From 1531, King Henry himself had been in touch with the Protestants of Germany, mainly seeking their help with his matrimonial affairs. However, seeking to enhance his own position regarding a possible Church Council, he considered joining the Smalcald Federation. They, in turn, requested that the King advance the Gospel and the true faith in England. When, finally,

---

9. Reu, *Sources*, 159

10. This divided Catholic/Protestant church only really broke down during the Second World with the migration of German refugees flooding all the German confessional states and the intermingling of their populations. Because of this turmoil—lasting effectively 500 years to the birth of post war Christian 'non-confessional' Germany it has been once again possible to resume a dialogue on the Articles of the Confession which never found agreement in the 16th Century.

the 39 Articles of the Church of England were being composed, they were influenced by the Augsburg Confession and discussions held in Wittenberg between Bishop Edward Fox with Luther, Melanchthon, Bugenhagen, Jonas and Cruziger.[11] The Anglican Church then became the Confession of the British Empire.

Consequent to the failure of Augsburg Diet to preserve Christian unity in Europe, Europe itself started to fall apart—both religiously and politically. This was not just between Lutheran states and Catholic states, but also with Calvinist territories and other smaller independent Anabaptist groups. The threads of the garment of unity in Europe, which had been stitched together by the Church over the centuries, were gradually being unwound, and sometimes torn and rent apart. Europe was becoming a continent of independent states, linguistically, politically and religiously. Whilst this 'coming apart' doubtless assisted in the creation of nation states with their internal creative dynamics, the unity of the Gospel, for which Christ prayed, was broken.

Did anything happen subsequently to help heal the Christian divide?

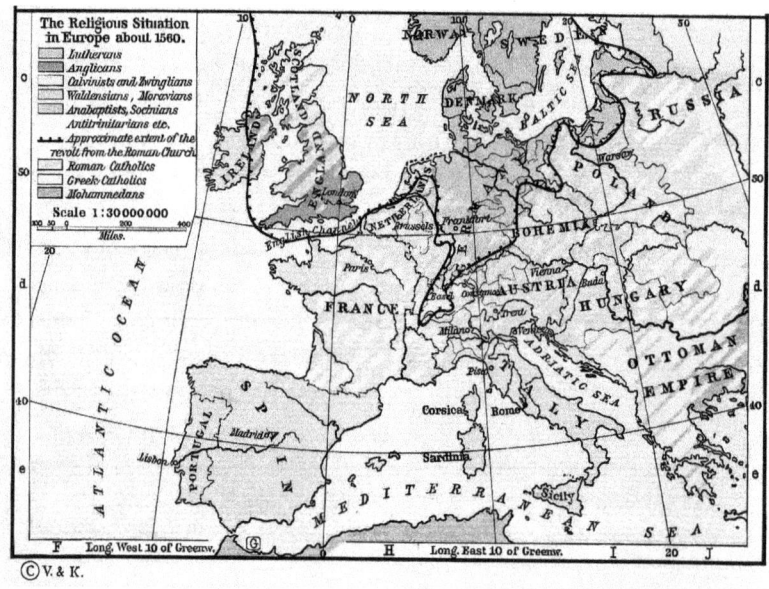

Map of Europe from 1560 showing religious divide

11. Reu, Sources,188ffl.

# 8

# Attempts at Reconciliation

## THE COUNCIL OF TRENT

THROUGHOUT THE PERIOD OF the Reformation there arose a passionate desire across the whole of Christendom for healing, Church reform and the revival of genuine spirituality. This was, however, resisted on both sides, by extreme curialism[1] on behalf of the Church and by the rising tide of Protestantism, unbridled from the power of Rome.[2] All in Germany—and not just Luther's followers—were clamoring for such a Council, while the Emperor feared that, without one, there would be a general apostacy across the Holy Roman Empire. Even in 1530 the Emperor Charles was completely convinced of the necessity for a general Church Council, feeling that without such a council, Germany would be lost to the Church. Schism had to be avoided at all costs, and to ensure this, France, England and Scotland would also have to be represented. In 1548, he wrote "In the midst of human vagaries but one universal rule—'trust in the help of the Almighty'. . .'to gain this one must defend our holy faith. After all my efforts and schemes to win back the Apostates of Germany, I have come to recognize that the Council is the only means."[3]

    1. The Doctrine of the Ultramontane section of the Catholic Church which places strong emphasis on the Powers and Position of the Pope and the Roman Curia,
    2. Lortz *Reformation*, 228
    3. Lortz *Reformation*, 229

## Una Sancta

The previous Lateran Council of 1512–17 renewed the Bull *Unam Sanctum*, where the Pope had been described as 'God upon Earth 'with consequent exalted spiritual powers. The Council had declared "As the Ark of the Covenant the rod and manna lay close to the table of the Law, so on the breast of the Pope knowledge of divine law lies close to the sword of destruction and the sweetness of grace."[4] Joseph Lortz described the Church as having "an unrestrained exaggeration of curialism' which was the biggest obstacle in finding common understanding with Protestantism. With such a papacy, it was said that 'people paid more heed to the laws of men than to the word of God.'"[5]

Charles himself was imbued with a deep churchman-like sense of solemn responsibility before God. He was aware of the important guiding role of the leaders of Church in the task of promoting Christ's Kingdom on earth in 'Christendom'. Finally, on December 28th, 1530, a decision was reached to call a Council.[6] This was just three months after the failure of the Reform movement and Church leaders to agree together at the Diet of Augsburg. Like any such event involving the whole of the European church, the Council itself was several years in organization, and in 1533, delegates led by Peter Paul Vergerio set off to seek out support and interest in the Council, including visiting the Reformers at Wittenberg.

Eck, who had opposed Melanchthon at Augsburg and had composed much of the *Confutato*, was now eager for a Council "as the one indispensable means of rooting out heresy."[7] In 1537 he continued to declare that "without a Council all of Germany, England, Denmark, Sweden and Norway would be forever lost. When would apostasy end?"[8] Eck was no stranger to Rome and had helped in the drafting of Luther's excommunication. He knew of the power and corruption of the Curia and of the lack of

---

4. 'Take care that we lose not that salvation, that life and breath which thou has given us, for thou art our Shepherd, thou are our physician, thou are our Governor, thou art our husbandman, thou are finally another God upon earth. Christopher Marcellus in oration addressed to Pope Julius II in the Fifth Lateran Council session IV (1512) Quoted in History of the Councils Vol XIV Col 109 by Labbe and Cossart and in

Lortz Joseph The Reformation in Germany Volume 2. Darton Longman and Todd London 1940 Trans. 1949 p.226

5. Lortz, *Reformation*, 227 Quoting Hoffmeister (1538)
6. Lortz, *Reformation*,.231
7. Lortz *Reformation*,231(1535)
8. Lortz *Reformation*,232

## Attempts at Reconciliation

integrity of many of the holders of the Papal Office. He was thus aware of the obstacles facing any Council. He wrote

> For twenty years we have been accustomed to such legations, burdened with mandates and articles and a tissue of obscure words, riddled with controversial points and conditions, couched in a labyrinth of equivocal phrases, so that Germans have been laughing for years at fine promises of a Council.[9]

If the Pope was not now seen to be in earnest about a Council, the hope of winning the Germans back to the church would be in vain. Like cascading dominoes, city after city and Duchy after Duchy in Germany were leaving the Church. Eck attributed the fault of this to the Church itself: "our sins have mounted so high that the world no longer deserves a Council, and so the whole structure of the Church will collapse."[10] Eck's hope for the Council was that it would in fact "reclaim the apostates." The question, however, was whether the German reformers themselves would attend the Council.

Vergerio travelled a second time to Wittenburg to invite the Reformers to attend and met and had dinner with Luther and Bugenhagen at the Elector's Castle. When a Bull was finally promulgated on July 2nd 1536, calling for the Council to meet on 23 May 1537 in Mantua, it was announced that the main aim of the Council would be to stamp out heresy. On hearing this, the Protestants immediately refused to be involved. Those who had supported the Reformation as a part of the Schmalkaldic League also refused any involvement with the Council. By this time Luther was seriously ill and poured out invective on the work of the Council and the Pope. Troubles also came with the Council which was prorogued in 1537 and 1538 before being permanently adjourned in 1539. Finally, a purely Catholic Council (without any person(s) representing the German reform movement) was called on March 15, 1545, to take place in Trent on the following December 13th. Its purpose was to affirm Catholic Doctrines and defend the Church from the Protestant Reformation

---

9. Lortz, *Reformation*, 232
10. Lortz, *Reformation*, .232

## THE COLLOQUY OF RATISBON IN REGENSBURG (1541)

The Colloquy of Ratisbon was a conference that was gathered to restore Christian Unity between the factions. It was held in 1541 at Regensburg in Bavaria, and was the final attempt before the Council to restore unity between Catholics and Protestants in the Holy Roman Empire, through a process of theological debate. The initial subject for debate was to be the *Augsburg Confession* with Melanchthon's *Apology* of the Augsburg Confession. However, at a secret conference between the Canon of Cologne, Johann Gropper and delegates from Protestant Strasbourg, the promise made to start discussions on the basis of the Augsburg Confession was rescinded. A new document, called the *Regensburg Book*, was chosen for debate instead. When Luther received a copy of the *Regensburg Book*, he decided that neither side would in fact be able to agree to its formulation. This became the last time for possible agreement between both sides to be established and it was noted that the *Confessio Augustana* was not to be debated and the colloquy ended without any agreement.[11] By that time the Confession had already been an accepted Christian confession for the reformed movement in Prussia, the Smalcald League, Saxony, Hesse, Braunschweig, Luneburg Anhalt, Köthen and Strasbourg as well as by King Christian of Denmark.

## THE COUNCIL OF TRENT (1545-1563)

The Council of Trent, when it arrived, was a monumental event in Church history. Called initially to respond to the Reformation in Germany, it sought to bring root and branch reform to the Church which had been seen to be weak in spirituality, too involved politically, with a highly exaggerated view of its own self-importance. It did much to create the character and structures for the modern church, nearly up to the advent of the Second Vatican Council. It restored church discipline, gave the motivation for a whole new wave of evangelization in North and South America, Africa and Asia as well as creating a whole new flowering of Catholic education at secondary and university level.

---

11. https://en.wikipedia.org/wiki/Diet_of_Regensburg_(1541) incorporating text from a publication in the public domain: T Kolde (1914). "Regensburg, Conference of". In Jackson, Samuel Macauley (ed.). *New Schaff–Herzog Encyclopedia of Religious Knowledge* (third ed.). London and New York: Funk and Wagnalls.

## Attempts at Reconciliation

According to Lortz, the fact that no Protestant groups attended the start of the Council did not mean that they had no interest in the events. On the contrary, they wanted to seek reasons to justify their non-attendance. The Council itself decided initially not to deal with questions of reform, but rather to start with contested articles of faith including the doctrine of Justification. For the German public it was a disappointment that reform was not top of the agenda, leaving little hope for restoring the unity of Christendom. When the Council moved to Bologna there was even less hope of resolving the 'German question' and the schism as the Council there no longer had any connections with the Emperor and the Empire, and the Council was run purely by 'non-imperial' fathers. The Council moved again back to Trent when the new Pope Julius III was elected. The Council was reconvened on 14th November 1550 and started again on 1 May 1551. This time, the German Bishops of Mainz, Trier, and Cologne were present, as well as procurators from Protestant Princes and Imperial Cities. The Germans were invited again to the Fifteenth session of the Council under Pope Julius. When the Council was prorogued, the decree now included reference to the Augsburg Confession and promised safe passage and the ability to discuss any matter or raise matters with the assembled Council:

> The holy, ecumenical and general Council of Trent, lawfully assembled in the Holy Ghost,... fully concedes the public faith and the fullest and truest security, which they call a safe-conduct, to each and all priests, electors, princes, dukes, marquises, counts, barons, soldiers, the common people... of the German province and nation, to the cities and other places thereof, and to all other ecclesiastical and secular persons, especially those of the Confession of Augsburg, who shall come or be sent with them to this general Council of Trent... to come freely to this city of Trent, to remain, abide and sojourn here and to propose, speak and consider, examine and discuss any matters whatever with the council, and to present freely whatever they may think suitable, to set forth any articles whatever either in writing or orally, and to explain, establish and prove them by the Sacred Scriptures and by the words, decisions and arguments of the blessed Fathers, and also to reply, if need be, to the objections of the general council, and to dispute and confer charitably and respectfully and without hindrance and respectfully with those who have been selected by the council, reproachful, vexatious and offensive language being absolutely put aside; and particularly, that the controverted matters shall be treated in this Council of Trent in accordance with

Sacred Scripture and the traditions of the Apostles, the approved councils, the consensus of the Catholic Church and the authority of the Holy Fathers . . .[12]

However, the possibility of any sort of reconciliation by this time had gone; the Council had already pronounced (with anathemas) on all basic issues of faith, contrasting sharply with every form of Protestant belief and theology. There were thus no fresh approaches to these questions at the third setting of the Council. Indeed, all the Protestants could do was to protest at the unfulfilled expectations and results. As Lortz pointed out: "The Council was powerless to alter anything in the political and ecclesial schism in religion in Germany. Its effects operated purely within the Catholic Church."[13]

The Decrees and Canons of the Council were subsequently promulgated to Churches across Europe. The Latin Edition of all the twenty-five sessions of the Council themselves were published much later by the Collegium Urbanum de Propaganda Fide in 1834. They included many chapters with Decrees and Canons to define Catholic belief and practice. The Decree on Justification itself was a central part of the work. The Council fathers had no decisions from earlier Council to help guide their work on Justification, and they spent seven months of arduous work formulating the decree on Justification. They drafted 33 Canons concerning the Doctrine, each given with a corresponding anathema.

How did the Catholic and Protestants world react to the results of the Council?

---

12. Schroeder, O.P *Canons and Decrees*, 116–17
13. Lortz, *Reformation*, 238

## Attempts at Reconciliation
# CATHOLIC AND PROTESTANT REACTIONS TO THE COUNCIL

**Martin Chemnitz Lutheran Theologian the 'Second Martin'.**

The results of the Council of Trent were contested right from the beginning. The first to start the contestation was Martin Chemnitz (1522–1586) who was a Lutheran Pastor and theologian of the second generation after Luther. He was nicknamed *Alter Martinus*—a 'Second Martin' and it was said about him that "If Martin Chemnitz had not come along, Luther would hardly have survived." Chemnitz was a theologian and an apologist for the Reform and had studied under both Luther and Melanchthon at Wittenberg University, and later lectured as a member of staff. He was largely responsible for the creation of the Book of Concord (1580) which—to the present day—is the summation of Lutheran beliefs and the standard work for the Lutheran Church. He was the first to draw swords while the Council was itself drawing to a close. In 1562, he wrote a book against the work of the Jesuits called *Theologicae Jesuitarum Prascipua Capita'* 'Theological Chapters of the Jesuits.*

**Diogo de Payva de Andrada Catholic Theologian, defender of the Council of Trent.**

To counter this work, a Portuguese priest called Diogo de Payva de Andrada (1528–1575) wrote a defense of the Council called *Decem libri orthodoxarum explicationum* – *Ten books of orthodox explanations*. Andrada had been appointed by King Sebastian of Portugal to the Council and was himself a Professor of Theology. Andrada used his book to attack the points Chemnitz had made.

The debate continued when Chemnitz countered with his most famous work called *Examen Concilii Tridentini—an Examination of the Council of Trent*. This was a colossal work of four volumes written and published over the years 1565–1573. It analyzed the Decrees and the Canons of the Council of Trent from a Lutheran point of view and contained 87 pages alone given to a critique of the Trent Decree written on Justification. To rebut this work, Andrara produced what is regarded as his greatest work called *Defensio Tridentinæ fidei catholicæ et integerrimæ quinque libris compræhensa aduersus hæreticorum detestabiles calumnias & præsertim Martini Kemnicij Germani*. This work translates as *A Defence of the Catholic and Most Sound Faith of the Council of Trent, in five books, against the Detestable Calumnies of Heretics, and especially those of Martin Chemnitz*. It was published—posthumously—in Portugal in 1578 and later translated in German and printed in Cologne (1580) and Ingolstadt (1592).[14]

These opposing theologians consequently supplied much of the material for the debate between Catholics and Lutherans which has continued right up to the 21st century. A modern history of the Trent Council from a Catholic perspective was written by German Hubert Jedin (1900–1980). He was a German priest, of part Jewish background, who fled to Rome during the war and lived at the Campo Santo Teutonico. Here he was under the protection of the Pope and was able to work on a history of the Council of Trent, His description of the Council ran to 2400 pages in four volumes . It was published in the years 1951–75. Chemnitz's work was translated to English by Lutheran seminary Professor Fred Kramer and was published in 1978. The debate regarding the Council and indeed the whole Reformation has never ceased since the time of the 16th century.

Was the Council of Trent itself counterproductive for reform?

Christopher Dawson in his seminal book *The Dividing of Christendom* summarized the positive achievements of the Council. He describes how the Council reestablished orthodoxy among the confusions of dogma and brought to bear fresh discipline in its ranks. The Council tackled the abuses which had affected Church governance, the question of non-residence of bishops, poor preaching and the inadequate level of clerical education. The Jesuits were, to Dawson, foundational in this regard, with the renewal of catechetics. Education both at school level and in seminaries was developed at this time, and this included higher studies in theology, philosophy and history. All of this was accompanied by a new mystic revival in 16th century Spain led by Saint Teresa of Avila, St John of the Cross and the work of the Carmelites which had its affect across the Catholic world.[15]

With this new self-confidence, new Mission fields for the Catholic Church were opened across the world to Asia, Africa and to the Americas. Countries in Europe such as Ireland and Poland now had their religious character shaped by the Council teachings. However, the possibility of acceptance by the Protestant world and the healing of the schism was impossible, as Protestant teachings were explicitly condemned from the start of the Council. Europe was still divided religiously, culturally as well as politically. As Germany itself was divided by the principle of *cujus regio, illus religio*, making each individual German state responsible for its

14. https://en.wikipedia.org/wiki/Diogo_de_Paiva_de_Andrade
15. Dawson, *Dividing of Christendom*, 131–33

religious teaching and character, meant that the Council was in no way representative of the whole European church. As the Council was predominantly Italian and Spanish in membership with a Latin-based culture, the communities of northern Europe of Germany and the Scandinavian Countries became alienated from the Catholic church culturally as well as theologically. The gulf between the Catholic south and the Protestant North of Europe became wider and wider over the next centuries leading, in the mind of Dawson, to the eventual secularization of the Western world.[16] The Council finally closed on December 4th 1563 now under the leadership of Pope Pius IV. An oration was given at the time, which said

> This most happy day has dawned for the Christian people; the day in which the temple of the Lord, often shattered and destroyed, is restored and completed, and this one ship, laden with every blessing and buffeted by the worst and most relentless storms and waves is brought safely to port.

While Pope Pius IV lauded the genuine achievements and reforms of the Council, he shows some genuine regret the non-attendance of the Reform movement. He believes however that no fault can be attributed to the Fathers for their absence at the Council

> Oh, that those for whose sake this voyage was chiefly undertaken had decided to board it with us; that those who caused us to take this work in hand had participated in the erection of this edifice! Then indeed we would now have reason for greater rejoicing. But it is certainly not through our fault that it so happened.[17]

While the Pope admits to some of the critiques of the Evangelicals of church discipline, he describes them as having "weak and infirm spirits". He sees them:

> in need of the explanation and confirmation of the Catholic and truly evangelical faith in those matters upon which they had cast doubt and which at this time appeared opportune for the dispersion and destruction of all the darkness of errors; the other the restoration of ecclesiastical discipline of which they claim was the chief cause of their severance from us, for we have amply

---

16. Dawson, *Dividing* of Christendom, 133–34
17. Schroeder O.P., Canons and Decrees, 259

accomplished both so far as was in our power and so far as the conditions of the times would permit.[18]

## READING HISTORY 'BACKWARDS'

While there is always a danger in reading documents such as the Decrees and Canons of Trent 'backwards' in the light of modern knowledge and understanding, it is still possible to suggest some areas in the conclusions of Trent which proved not so beneficial in hindsight: this was especially true regarding any work of ecumenism. Towards the end of the Council in the 25th session, ten rules were given concerning "prohibited books." These rules were drawn up by the Council Fathers and approved by Pope Pius. In this area the Council adopted a very strict line. Often, under penalties, it stated:

> the works of heresiarchs. . . as well as of those who are or have been the leaders of heretics, as Luther, Zwingli, Calvin, Balthasar, Friedberg, Schwenkfeld[19] and others like these, whatever be their name, title or nature of their heresy are absolutely forbidden. The books of other heretics, however which deal professedly with religion are absolutely condemned.[20]

Max Lackmann (1910–2000), a pastor of the post war *Sammlung* ecumenical Lutheran movement, regretted the lack of knowledge which Catholics and Protestants had of each other. He said that this knowledge gap led to prejudice "which falsifies and renders unintelligible what happened and is supposed to have happened at the time of the schism".[21] While one might understand the Church Fathers did not want to teach what the reformers wrote, it would seem that very few people at all were permitted to join the argument or discussion to see what things might be held in common between the Church and the Reformers or indeed what each could learn from each other. One could reasonably suggest that this lack of ecumenical knowledge of different confessional writings certainly has continued to today in the 21st century and this legacy could be traced back to the Council.

---

18. Schroeder, O.P *Canons and Decrees*, 259–60
19. Caspar Schwenkfeld (1489–1561) was a radical Protestant reformer who lived in Silesia before being exiled as a heretic. Balthasar Hubmaier(1480–528) was an Anabaptist leader.
20. Schroeder, O.P., *Canons and Decrees*, 273
21. Lackmann, *Augsburg Confession*, 1

Regarding Biblical studies the rule stated:

> of writers, also ecclesiastical, which have till now been edited by condemned authors are permitted provided they contain nothing contrary to sound doctrine. The translations of the books of the Old Testament may in the judgment of the bishop be permitted to learned and pious men only, provided such translations are used only as elucidations of the Vulgate Edition for the understanding of the Holy Scriptures and not as the sound text. Translations of the New Testament made by authors of the first class of this list shall be permitted to no one, since great danger and little usefulness usually results to readers from their perusal. But if with such translations as are permitted or with the Vulgate Edition some annotations are circulated, these may also, after the suspected passages have been expunged by the theological faculty of some Catholic university or by the general inquisition, be permitted to those to whom the translations are permitted.[22]

According to this rule, reading of the scripture of any type was highly restricted to "learned and pious men" or to those "whom translations were permitted." This was coupled with the suggestion that "great danger and little usefulness would come from such perusal" of the Scripture in translation. Reading of general scriptural material was to be tightly controlled, often with spiritual and even material penalties: The Church Fathers were obviously very concerned about the spread of any heresy and sectarianism and the corruption of dogma.

> Since it is clear from experience that if the Sacred Books are permitted everywhere and without discrimination in the vernacular, there will by reason of the boldness of men arise therefrom more harm than good, the matter is in this respect left to the judgment of the bishop or inquisitor, who may with the advice of the pastor or confessor permit the reading of the Sacred Books translated into the vernacular by Catholic authors to those who they know will derive from such reading no harm but rather an increase of faith and piety, which permission they must have in writing. Those, however, who presume to read or possess them without such permission may not receive absolution from their sins till they have handed them over to the ordinary. Book dealers who sell or in any other way supply Bibles written in the vernacular to anyone who has not this permission, shall lose the price of the books, which is to be applied by the bishop to pious purposes, and

---

22. Schroeder O.P. *Canons and Decrees*, 274

## Attempts at Reconciliation

> in keeping with the nature of the crime they shall be subject to other penalties which are left to the judgment of the same bishop. Regulars who have not the permission of their superiors may not read or purchase them.[23]

Times have undoubtedly changed, and all these Rules would strongly contrast from the exhortation given in the Second Vatican Council in the Document Dei Verbum, which stated:

> The sacred synod also earnestly and especially urges all the Christian faithful, especially Religious, to learn by frequent reading of the divine Scriptures the "excellent knowledge of Jesus Christ" (Phil. 3:8). 'For ignorance of the Scriptures is ignorance of Christ.' Therefore, they should gladly put themselves in touch with the sacred text itself, whether it be through the liturgy, rich in the divine word, or through devotional reading, or through instructions suitable for the purpose and other aids which, in our time, with approval and active support of the shepherds of the Church, are commendably spread everywhere.[24]

Whereas one might suggest therefore for various reasons that such Bible reading, study and devotion is more common among churches of other confessions, it is less common within Catholicism. One could reasonably connect this perceived weakness as a consequence of some of the Decrees of the Council of Trent.

One further area which was addressed by both the Vatican and Trent Councils was the practice of the use of the Vernacular in the Liturgy. At the twenty second Session of the Trent Council, the Council Fathers stated under the heading: "The Mass may not be celebrated in the Vernacular. Its mysteries to be explained to the people" –

> Though the mass contains much instruction for the faithful, it has, nevertheless not been deemed advisable by the Fathers that it should be celebrated everywhere in the Vernacular tongue.[25]

The arguments given at the Second Vatican Council for the use of the Vernacular in the Liturgy would however echo the thoughts of the Reformers. Chemnitz wrote in his Examination of the Council of Trent

---

23. Schroeder, O.P. *Canons and Decrees*, 274–75
24. Flannery O.P. *Vatican II Documents Dei Verbum*, 764
25. Schroeder O.P. *Canons and Decrees*, 148

> For where has God revealed that the dignity of the Latin language is so great that the Holy Scripture should be read only in it? God certainly does not want his doctrine to be known only to Latin people. If, therefore, the command of God is to transmit and proclaim the doctrine of the New Testament to the peoples of all languages so that they can understand, this certainly cannot be done unless the doctrine of the Scripture is in the proclamation translated into those languages which are known to the peoples to whom Christ is to be preached... For the languages of all nations have been sanctified by the Holy Spirit that they may sound forth the wonderful works of God...'[26]

Melchite Patriarch Maximos Saigh expressed similar sentiments to at the Second Vatican Council:

> without doubt Christ spoke to his contemporaries in their own language. He used a language which was understandable to all his hearers namely Aramaic, when he celebrated the first eucharistic sacrifice. The apostles and disciples acted likewise. It would never have occurred to them that the celebrant in a Christian assembly should read the passages of scripture, should sing the Psalms, should preach or break the bread using a different language than that of the congregation.'[27]

Although much progress was made at the Trent Council to reform the institution of the Church, we are, at this stage, a long way from any reconciliation between the two parts of the 16th century schism in the Western Church. In the intervening period between Trent and the modern era there were occasional colloquies between Catholic and Lutheran theologians. Despite any prohibitions on reading the works of the Reformers, scholars were reading them and debating their contents. One of the most interesting, involved Fr. Robert Bellarmine SJ (1542–1621) and Lutheran theologian Johann Gerhard (1582–1637). Gerhard's chief work was a multi-volume exposition called *Loci Communes theologici*, which debated the writings of Bellarmine. In turn, Bellarmine gave his own defense of his own writings, supportive of the Council of Trent and challenged the views of Gerhard. Timothy Wengert and Sister Susan Wood in the Book *A Shared Spiritual Journey* say that:

---

26. Chemnitz *Examination of the Council of Trent*,.200–201
27. Fr. Joseph Ratzinger/Pope Benedict XVI *Highlights of Vatican II* 36

although both theologians were apologists—by no stretch of imagination ecumenists—they represented an important first phase in ecumenical rapprochement: careful listening to the arguments of the other side. Even though the conversations ended in condemnation, the fact that such exchanges took place at all signaled to their age and ours just how important divisions in the church were for them.[28]

---

28. Wood K. Susan and Wengert Timothy J A Shared Spiritual Journey,.32

# 9

# The Healing of the Divide

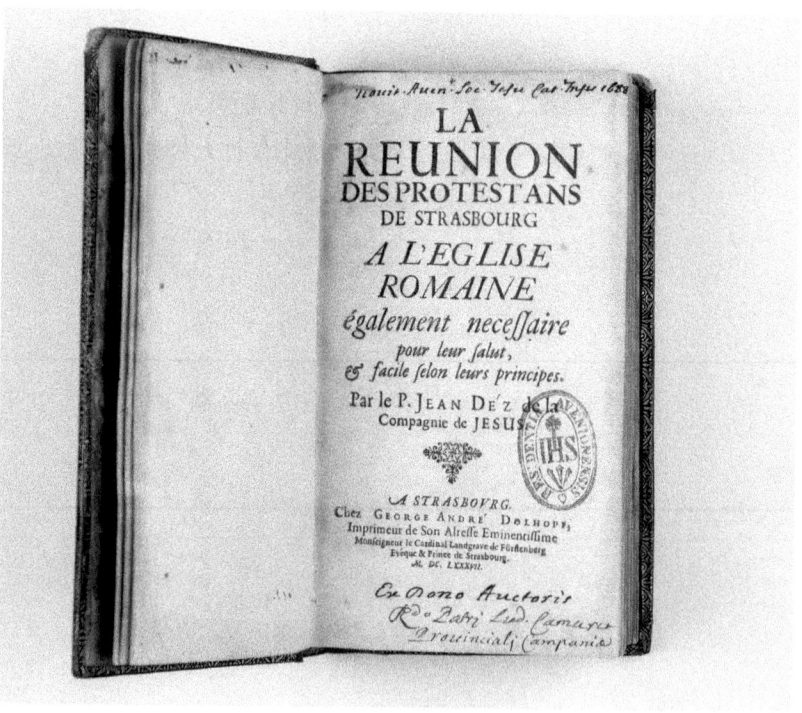

1688 Book of Fr. Jean Dez S.J. who argued reunion of Strasbourg Protestants
was "easy according to their teaching" in the Augsburg Confession

## The Healing of the Divide

Following the split which happened due to the failure to agree at Augsburg the two parts of the church started to drift further and further apart. In Germany they were separated politically, legally, geographically, as well as spiritually and religiously. One outsider who tried to bring them back together in the 17th Century was Father Jean Dez, a French Jesuit, who wrote a book of over 600 pages, examining the teaching of the Augsburg Confession from a Roman Catholic point of view. It was published in Strasbourg in 1688 in two editions, in French and German. His conclusion, following a long examination of the Confession, was that the "reunion of the Protestants of Strasbourg with the Catholic church is necessary for their salvation and easy according to their teaching".[1] The title was indeed revolutionary and vitally important for the City of Strasbourg, which had experienced the *Bishop's war*. This was a conflict between Catholics and Protestant for the control of the Bishopric of Strasbourg; it was one of only two outbreaks of sectarian conflict that occurred between the Peace of Augsburg in 1555 and the outbreak of the Thirty Years War in 1618.[2] Dez's call for unity was thus highly practical and both necessary spiritually and "easy according to their teaching." It is not clear if Fr. Dez's appeal succeeded in any meaningful way, given that the Europe was still recovering from all the scars of the 30 years' war (1618–1648), which pitted Catholics and Protestants against each other across Europe. As we will see later, his analysis of the Augsburg Confession and his consequent hopes for a reconciliation of the schism entered the conversations of the 20th century; at this time the whole division of the church was revisited by scholars and writers. The effects of the conflict had moved the two sides farther apart, in what might have seemed like an impassable divide. Both sides were still following their own narratives regarding the cause of the schism. There was no discernible movement of reconciliation between that time and the 20th century, approximately 350 years later.

## THE BIRTH OF THE ECUMENICAL MOVEMENT

The first move towards Christian unity between Protestant groups was at the time of the famous *Edinburgh and the World Missionary Conference*

---

1. Lackmann Catholic Unity ,32 referencing Fr Jean Dez SJ, *La reunion des Protestants de Strasbourg a l'Eglise romaine également necessaire pour leur salut, et facile selon leurs principes* ( Strasbourg 1687)

2. https://en.wikipedia.org/wiki/Strasbourg_Bishops%27_War

which sought to bring together missionary activities from the array of Protestant Confessions. The largest Protestant and Church of England missionary societies, coming from across North America and Europe, sent over 1200 delegates to Edinburgh with what was the start of the modern Ecumenical Movement.[3] This work, however, did not involve the Catholic community, but it did create an ecumenical wave that eventually started to flow between the two churches of the Reformation. To bridge the divide required understanding, inspiration, courage, and work from both sides.

The Holy Spirit inspired two main movements in Germany to work from both sides for the dream of Christian Unity, with quite a degree of success. This success did not appear immediately,—but as both sides started to normalize relations following the trauma of the second world war, they created a move which made deeper reconciliation possible. The two groups were the *Una Sancta Brotherhood* of Blessed Max Josef Metzger (1887–1944) and the *Sammlung* Gathering of Lutheran Pastors and Leaders. Both started to work on that painstaking call to remove all the debris of misinformation and prejudice which had separated them for so long.

## DIE SAMMLUNG: THE GATHERING

In the time before the Vatican Council (1963–65), non-Catholic Christians were spoken of by the Holy Office of the Catholic Church as being 'schismatics and heretics'.[4] Although the church had always wished to reconcile with the Orthodox after the East-West split of 1054, and to the Lutherans and Protestants at the time of the Reformation, the only way of achieving this at that time was for the other Christians to 'return to Rome'. Rev. Hans Asmussen, a German Lutheran pastor, posed a question to then Roman Catholic Archbishop Augustin Bea in 1947 when Bea was Rector of the Pontifical Biblical Institute. He said "Rome is always speaking of the need for the Protestants to 'return'". "What would happen if I brought the news that Protestants were returning tomorrow?" The reply was given by Bea. "That would be tricky since Rome is not prepared for it." Asmussen was a leader in the Confessing Church, and he had been jailed several times for his outspoken opposition to Hitler and the Third Reich. He was not afraid to challenge Bea for his response and said: "In that case, the appeal

---

3. https://en.wikipedia.org/wiki/1910_World_Missionary_Conference
4. Schmidt *Augustin Bea*, 237.

to return is irresponsible, an empty formula and the expression of the old lust for power."[5]

Asmussen and many other Lutheran Clergy had been deeply affected by Hitler and the Third Reich and had suffered for the witness of their faith. Hitler desired to create a purely German Reich Church under the authority of the State which 'would exclude all those deemed impure and embrace all 'true Germans' in a spiritual homeland for the Third Reich.' The Nazi leadership had chosen Bishop Ludwig Müller for this purpose, and, in a vote in 1933, two thirds of Protestant Christians supported him to become its leader.[6] A fellow Lutheran pastor of Asmussen, Max Lackmann had also fallen foul of the Third Reich and had been sent to Dachau Concentration Camp. Here he was interned with many Catholic priests, an experience which had a profound effect on his life. After his release from Dachau, he decided to dedicate himself to the cause of ecumenism. In January 1954 Asmussen and Lackmann, together with two other Lutheran clergymen Ernst Fincke and Wolfgang Lehmann, founded a movement called *Die Sammlung*—a word meaning 'the Gathering'. Together they felt a divine call to reunite divided Christendom, which had suffered so much during the War. Archbishop Bea took an interest in the development of the group and studied Asmussen's Book *Rom, Wittenberg Moskau,* which was published in 1956. He found that he was able to agree with many of Asmussen's conclusions, and later Asmussen visited Bea in Rome to discuss his work. He was deeply impressed by the Archbishop. Asmussen, too, was encouraged by his time with the Archbishop, and wrote up and circulated his written impressions of this to fifty leading figures, including sending a copy to the Archbishop. The Archbishop also wished to 'keep the dialog going'; Asmussen and Bea continued with their discussion, with Bea responding subsequently with eleven pages of reflections.[7]

*Die Sammlung* movement started to spread. Meetings and retreats were held and works published. The most significant publication was entitled *Katholische Reformation,* which was published in 1957, and later translated into English in 1961 as *The Unfinished Reformation'—Twelve Evangelical Affirmations of Catholic Truths.* The first edition of the book

---

5. Wolfgang Lehmann, Hans Asmussen p.121-22 as quoted in Stjepan Schmidt '*Augustin Bea* 'Footnote to p.240.

6. https://www.facinghistory.org/resource-library/protestant-churches-nazi-state Accessed 12/13/24

7. Schmidt *Augustin Bea,* 240–41

produced 20,000 widely written copies. In Germany and in Italy, it received favorable reviews by both Catholics and Protestants. The leading Catholic paper in Italy, *Il Quotidiano* wrote concerning the book under a striking heading "The End of the Reformation?". The Catholic paper *Rheinischer Merkur* wrote in its edition of August 2 1957, "Behind the Twelve theses there is obviously a burning, spiritual passion for the unity of the Church, and behind this passion are men and women, active ,striving Christians, all of one mind and purpose, regardless of creed." The *Allgemeine Sonntag Zeitung* of Würzburg in an edition of July 7th 1957 declared " The publishing of these Theses also made its impact upon us Catholics, penetrating to our very hearts."[8]

In the book, the five leading members of the Sammlung—authors Hans Asmussen, Max Lackmann, Ernst Fincke, Richard Baumann and Wolfgang Lehmann, stated that:

> we must face the question of truth more earnestly than ever before, and we must acknowledge that Reformation doctrine and likewise our whole ecclesiastical life are heavily weighed with mis- judgements on both sides...therefore a mutual acknowledgement must be made and a new relationship established with the pre-Reformation Catholic church, for we owe it to the welfare of the whole church to make such acknowledgement. Only in proportion as we take the question of truth seriously can we hope to overcome the differences between the churches as well as those within Protestantism itself.[9]

When they started in 1954, *Die Sammlung* was quite alone in purpose and vision, and had to face the knowledge that every serious approach to the Catholic Church was viewed as 'a denial of faith.'[10] Most Lutherans regarded that, after the Peace of Augsburg in 1555, evangelicals were finished with the Catholic Church. However, the *Sammlung* members were encouraged by hopeful signs in the Church hierarchies, which signaled a new possible rapprochement. In doing so, Lutherans were having to admit that the Lutheran Church of 1530 was much more 'Catholic' than it was in their day, leading to the point of whether Lutherans then (of the 1950's) still believed in the tenets that were espoused in the Augsburg Confession. For example, one article in the Confession (no. XXVIII) taught that, "by divine

---

8. Asmussen Ed *The Unfinished Reformation* Preface xxxiv
9. Asmussen Ed *The Unfinished Reformation* Preface, xxxv
10. Asmussen Ed. *The Unfinished Reformation*, 4

right, bishops have the power of jurisdiction in matters of faith and morals." However, *Sammlung* leaders pointed to the fact that there had been no such episcopal practice in the Lutheran Churches for the previous 400 years; those who would still wish to hold to the principles of the CA would thus be classed as 'being Catholic'. This was in spite of Melanchthon's Apology being a completely Catholic exposition of the Evangelical cause. The main way traditional Lutherans viewed the differences between Catholics and Evangelicals was by a simple formula: Evangelicals believed in 'justification by faith', while Catholics believed they were 'sanctified by good works.' The *Sammlung* were therefore pleased to declare that the famous letter between evangelical Karl Barth and Catholic theologian Hans Küng on this doctrine had finally dealt with this "inglorious period of inter-church polemics and debate."[11] The *Sammlung* thus refused such categorizing; the actual situation was much more complex and needed careful analysis and debate. Any such dialogue needed to be exercised in an atmosphere of love and respect.

The *Sammlung* viewed that the Lutheran Reformation was meant to be a 'corrective' within the Catholic Church. They stated:

> If this corrective becomes a fixed condition, then it will bring about the very undoing of the church…this is unquestionably true for we can never be rid of the Catholic Church…we came forth from this Church, and within her communion alone can we find our fulfillment. In the measure this occurs we will also accomplish our corrective mission. In the same degree will a Catholic Reformation be finally achieved.'[12]

In the seven circular letters to other members and supporters of the movement, they share their concern with a wider audience. They see that the era of the Church vacillating is due to a lack of unity, and that the Lutheran Church should not regard it as though the Church itself did not exist prior to 1517. Their newsletters were sent across Germany to seek others of like mind who saw the rupture in what "should have been an indissoluble link between Christ and His Church, between Creation and supernatural Grace, between Holy Scripture and the history of the Church. This had resulted, they said, in diminishing the authority of the Lord and the power of grace and scripture in the Evangelical Church."[13] Their conferences—which

---

11. https://postbarthian.com/2014/08/04/karl-barths-letter-endorsing-hans-kungs-justification/
12. Asmussen *The Unfinished Reformation*, 15
13. Asmussen *The Unfinished Reformation*, 26

sometimes attracted as many as 800 participants—dealt with difficult and sometimes painful subjects, which helped those on the verge of giving up. Many attending were visibly moved by the contribution of Catholic partners. They were thus prepared to accept the reproach of those who would not countenance such fellowship with Catholics, in the belief that 'only that which is universally Christian is Christian at all. That which is Catholic is Christian; whatever is merely partial or local is not Christian'.[14]

The subjects of the actual theses in the book were wide ranging and controversial: "the Church's Christian mysteries, the relation of Grace and Freedom, the sacrifice of Christ, the apostolic succession of bishops, the office of priesthood and ordination, the primacy of the chair of Peter, the Episcopal teaching office, the relation of Scripture and tradition and the importance of the veneration of the saints in the life of the Church."[15] The German publisher said that the significance of the book "is the call for a Catholic Reformation in the Evangelical Church and likewise for a renewal of Catholicity in the Roman Church in the spirit of the evangelical tradition."[16]

Archbishop Bea took considerable time studying the twelve theses, and discussed it on several occasions, drawing up a list of comments and observations amounting to several pages. He made mention of the movement in his own book on Ecumenism, *The Unity of Christians*.[17] Looking back from the vantage of 2025, it could easily be surmised that the work had some significant influence upon the Council and the reforms that took place after it, "creating this renewal of Catholicity in the Roman Church in the Spirit of the evangelical tradition."[18] The Second Vatican Council was only summoned in 1959, two years after the publishing of *Die Sammlung's Katholische Reformation*. It was a complete surprise that the new 'caretaker' Pope should call for such a major event in church history and open it successfully to other churches to attend and even participate. The work of *Die Sammlung*, together with the *Una Sancta Brotherhood* of Fr Max Metzger, helped to create the atmosphere for such an epochal defining event in the history of the church.

Later in 1962, while the Council was just starting, the now 'Cardinal' Bea visited Heidelberg as the President of the *Secretariat for Promoting*

---

14. Asmussen *The Unfinished Reformation* 52
15. Asmussen *The Unfinished Reformation*, Intro., xxxiv
16. Asmussen *The Unfinished Reformation*, Intro, xxxiv
17. Cardinal Bea *The Unity of Christians*.43 Footnote
18. Asmussen *The Unfinished Reformation* Intro xxxiv

*Christian Unity* to talk about the Council and the prospects for Christian Unity. He met up once again with his Lutheran friend Hans Asmussen. Cardinal Bea's secretary Stjepan Schmidt recalls Asmussen as saying "Now that your secretariat is undertaking what I was aiming at, I can retire."[19] In 1963, the *Die Sammlung* movement ceased meeting, whilst some,—including Max Lackmann,—continued with the *Association for Evangelical Catholic Reunion*. None of the leaders of *Die Sammlung* wished to convert to Catholicism. They wished to remain faithful to their own Lutheran tradition, and to work for reconciliation between the churches. Sadly, they were sidelined; their pioneering work had helped to prepare the way for the Vatican Council and over thirty years later for the *Joint Declaration on the Doctrine of Justification*. Hans Asmussen retorted to the accusations of wishing to be Catholic saying: "I have no Catholizing tendencies, but rather a Catholic passion."[20]

---

19. https://www.augsburg2030.org/augsburg-day-1930.html
20. Asmussen *The Unfinished Reformation*, 196

# 10

# Max Lackmann
## Author of 'The Augsburg Confession and Catholic Unity"

MAX LACKMANN, (1910–2000) LUTHERAN pastor and one of the founding members of *Die Sammlung*, was himself able to attend the Vatican Council as a non-participant observer. After returning from the opening session as the official representative of the *League for Evangelical-Catholic Reunion*, he decided that there was a real need for Catholic bishops, theologians and priests to better acquaint themselves with the *Augsburg Confession*, in order to consider the statements and problems of the first doctrinal Confessions of the Lutheran Reformation. He decided to re-issue a volume for this purpose called *The Augsburg Confession and Catholic Unity*. It was first published in 1959, just before the Council began and later published in English in 1963.[1] The book consisted of a series of talks he gave as a Lutheran minister to convocations of Roman Catholic religious orders, seminars for priests and pastoral conferences in Vienna, Graz, Münster, Sieburg and the Cistercian Cloister of the Holy Cross in Lower Austria.

In the introduction to the book, he regretted the lack of knowledge which separated Christians had of each other. He claimed that the 'other's names'—such as 'Protestant' or 'Catholic'- are "already burdened with

---

1. Lackmann, Max, *The Augsburg Confession and Catholic Unity*. Herder and Herder 1963 Translation Katholische Einheit und Augsburger Konfession Graz Styria Verlag 1959.

the mortgage of a polemic which falsifies and renders unintelligible what happened and is supposed to have happened four centuries ago."[2] In his book and talks, Lackmann wished to show (contrary to popular belief and understanding) that "the Confessors of Augsburg wanted to be Catholic Christians in the Western Roman Catholic Church", and why this "self-evident" desire foundered. He wished for both Catholics and Lutherans to concern themselves seriously with the Augsburg Confession and Melanch-thon's Apology, with the high goal of "overcoming the schism of the one Holy Church according to the Lord's will."

**Rev. Max Lackmann Founding member of Die Sammlung**

Max was re-issuing his book while participating in the Council called for by Pope Saint John XXIII, seeing the Council as a sign that the work of

2. Lackmann, *Catholic Unity*, 1

untying some of the knots and falsehoods of history had indeed already started. The Augsburg Confession itself appealed ungently for such a "general (ecumenical) free and Christian Council in order that the matters in dissention be settled and brought to Christian Concord in Western Christendom."[3] Lackmann states that the Council was a "long time coming in the 16th century," and that, when it actually began at Trent in 1545, it was in fact too late: one side—the Evangelicals—had then refused to participate. However, the desire for such a Council, first announced by Melanchthon in 1546, had never been retracted by Evangelical Christians: "We readily and wholeheartedly desire, indeed we pray God most sincerely, that a free Christian Council might be held."[4] Such a Council, he hoped, might be able to solve the problems which the one Western Church of the 16th century "could not solve without dividing into two denominations". For this, he declares, such a study and reappraisal of the Augsburg Confession and its Apology was indispensable. However, he sees this exercise as being a costly one:

> It will be costly for everyone who accompanies Jesus Christ as he goes about burning down the ancient walls which can no longer separate brethren. For *Confessio*[5] is simultaneously a confession of guilt and a praise to God. Both aspects of *Confessio* exact their pound of flesh from everyone who here accompanies the 'author and finisher of our faith'. The Confessors of Augsburg still knew about this cost.[6]

Lackmann himself paid a price for his foray into the heart of ecumenical endeavor; during the writing of his book, he was forced to surrender his pastoral ministry to his congregation, with his writing work being subject to a doctrinal examination—an almost unheard-of procedure in the Evangelical Church. He thus concludes that "in the realm of scholarship as in every other, one comes to salvation only through the cross."[7] In his scholarly work and talks, Lackmann argues that Christians belong together and cannot escape from each other, as all are routed in holy Baptism in the name of the Father, the Son, and the Holy Ghost. They are also united in

---

3. Lackmann *Catholic Unity* ,4
4. Lackmann, *Catholic Unity* , 5
5. The word 'Confessio', together with Confessio Augustana, AC and CA are shorthand for the Augsburg Confession.
6. Lackmann, Catholic Unity, 6
7. Lackmann, Catholic Unity, 9 quoting Dominican priest Fr. A.D. Sertillanges.

the historic Christian tradition through the outpouring of the Holy Spirit, developed into the Western Roman Catholic Church, with the Chair of St Peter becoming the center of God's people.[8]

> We would not have the Holy Scriptures, the Apostolic and Nicene Creeds, baptism and Holy Communion, fundamental dogmas and—self-evidently—Christian forms, rites and customs (e.g. The Church and its organizations, the Church Year, the Liturgy) if we had not received them through *this* Western Catholic Church, through her Councils, Popes, Bishops, missionaries, monks and theologians. We are the sons and daughters of *one* Holy Mother Church.[9]

The Augsburg Confession is, to Lackmann, to be viewed as originally a witness to the faith of the Catholic Church, "the concern of the whole world-wide- Catholic Church."[10] As Melanchthon stated, "we confess only the unadulterated, ancient, genuine teaching of the Christian Catholic Church. In order that everyone to know what such teaching is, we have publicly expressed it in the Augsburg Confession…which contains a briefly written summary of our teaching, and which is, without a doubt, in full agreement with the ancient symbols of the apostles, the Nicene Creed and St Athanasius."[11] The Augsburg Confession to the time of his writing (and indeed to the present time) is the binding proclamation for the church's teaching and proclamation. Lackmann agreed with Jesuit Fr. Jean Dez who wrote (as we alluded earlier) in his book of 1688 "it is unnecessary to be detained by the private opinions of one or another teacher". Again, quoting Marburg Lutheran A.F.C. Vilmar "the evangelical church must declare as a fundamental error the use of 'The Evangelical Confession' in the singular sense to describe a schism in the church which was intended or desired by evangelicals." According to its own understanding, the Evangelical Confession contains a universal churchly *Catholic* experience in the most eminent sense, which is the necessary crown of all experiences which, up to this time, has been received by the church and expressed in confessions.[12] This goes against the idea already present at the time of Dez who said [of Evangelicals] that "each one could believe what he especially preferred; for each

---

8. Lackmann, Catholic Unity, 11
9. Lackmann Catholic Unity, 12
10. Lackmann, Catholic Unity, 36
11. Lackmann, Catholic Unity, 37
12. Lackman, *Catholic Unity*, 38

interprets Scripture in his own way."[13] Lackmann therefore states that the Augsburg Confession is and remains valid as a Catholic symbol, a normative statement of Catholic doctrine.

Lackmann concludes because of these truths, however they formulate it, Evangelicals and Catholics are also members of this one holy Catholic Church. However, the churches of the Reformation failed in the task of manifesting and maintaining that unity of faith in God and in His Church; both are guilty of the 'offense of schism' and should earnestly desire unity. Speaking to his own Evangelical Church, he suggests that, if it does not seek that unity, it must view the church as "a sect without history, uncatholic and unapostolic"—which would be totally contrary to how Lutherans have always regarded themselves. He sees this quest for unity as being the desire of the Catholic Church, as Pope Pius IX, stated "the whole world will never know true peace until there is one flock and one shepherd."[14]

Lackmann saw the Vatican Council as now making this task 'a duty' for the church, and, as a part of this duty, he sees the necessity for Catholics "to know more about the Evangelical church: about its history; about the appeal of the Holy Spirit to its conscience; about its Catholic responsibility then and now."[15] This would be opposed to the [former, Catholic] one-sided 'confessionalistic' attitude of toward the 'erring sons' in the 'darkness of error'.[16] Instead of treating evangelicals as heretics, he asks " Is it not time for the Roman Catholic Church to see that the case for Protestantism—however one might classify it from the Roman Catholic viewpoint in the category of heresy—is historically, religiously, and theologically a *special* case in Western Christianity, and that one cannot do justice to it with what for centuries has been the normal attitude of the church?"[17] He then quotes [Lutheran] Bishop Stählin who said "in every—ism lies the motif of exclusiveness and intolerance . . . . a renunciation of polarity and wholeness, a one-dimensional opposition to every perspective to the depth and fullness of divine dimension."[18] By abandoning aloofness, "one will see how much and how far the phenomenon 'Evangelical' originates as a Catholic, yes even as a *Roman Catholic* phenomenon and wants to be so

---

13. Lackmann, *Catholic Unity*, 39
14. Lackmann, Catholic Unity, 15
15. Lackmann, *Catholic Unity,*18
16. Lackmann, *Catholic Unity*, 24
17. Lackmann, *Catholic unity*, .25
18. Lackmann *Catholic Unity*, 25

understood."[19] He cannot see that the Catholic task of the Reformation is finished: it was not finished by the Council of Trent, nor could it be by a mechanical general conversion to Roman Catholicism. On the contrary, the Evangelical existence can only find its true destiny and its true being when it is received and receivable as its own self by the Catholic Church. For this to happen repentance is necessary; if this is the correct ecumenical view of the Reformation, the schism, and the movement towards reunion, then the customary concepts of 'heretics' and 'return to the Church' are no longer adequate for Roman Catholicism's dealing with the problem of reunion.[20] Indispensable, too, he sees is looking afresh at the document which became the basis of the Lutheran Confessions,—the Augsburg Confession,—which remains an unfinished task. Dedication to this work would be an indispensable condition for avoiding all hasty and inappropriate reunion attempts and help prepare for the return of Evangelical Christianity (quoting Pius IX) to "the truth and fellowship with the Catholic Church."[21]

However, Lackmann notes that historically the Augsburg Confession has lost its central place in much Lutheran/Evangelical theology, and that many professional chairs have long abandoned the AC as a central reference point. He sees, however, such groups as the *Lutheran World Federation* and the *Evangelical Brotherhood of Saint Michael* regaining the sense of doctrinal formula and a teaching office for the church. In the rest of his exposition of the Augsburg Confession, Lackmann lists six theses for theological consideration:

1. The Confessio Augustana is recognized by the Evangelical Regional Churches, which are descended from the Lutheran Reformation, as a binding norm for ecclesiastical and apostolic teaching, preaching and the interpretation of scripture.

2. The Confessio Augustana contains a Catholic Confession to the ancient Catholic and apostolic deposit as it is presented in the Roman Catholic Church.

3. The Confessio Augustana condemns and rejects the ancient heresies as well as the 'pseudo-Catholicism' of medieval theology and folk piety which the Roman Catholic Church also condemns and rejects as un-Christian and un-Catholic.

---

19. Lackmann, *Catholic Unity*, 26
20. Lackmann, Catholic Unity, 27
21. Lackmann, *Catholic Unity,* 23

4. The Confessio Augustana contains new Catholic doctrinal experiences and theological insights which belong to the Catholic Church. They are based on ancient Catholic doctrinal experiences and theological insights of the Church. Their Catholic appropriation and assimilation is as much as ever, the task of the Roman Catholic Church.

5. The Confessio Augustana clearly adduces anti-Roman and anti-Catholic negatives which dispute and structurally alter the doctrine and form of the Western Church. These negatives are advanced as demands of the Gospel, the Holy Scriptures and the traditional faith of the Catholic Church in its earliest centuries. A confrontation with these negatives is still today the task of the Roman Catholic Church.

6. All the statements of the Confessio Augustana are related to the Roman Catholic Church. The CA is meant to be a Catholic contribution to the Catholic Church. At the same time this contribution resulted in the dissolution of Catholic unity. We must therefore investigate the un-Catholic presuppositions upon which the pros and cons of both confessors and opponents of the CA were based, and which meant that a solution could be found only in the un-Catholic confessional disunity of Western Christians.[22]

We have covered most of the first three theses in our preamble: the CA stands for the orthodoxy of the Roman Catholic Church tradition and does not see itself as a 'new church of the Reformation' or a new denomination. The remaining three theses deserve some elucidation and clarification. The fourth of the theses says the CA and the Evangelical experiences have insights which belong to the whole Catholic Church. He believes that the Council of Trent did not grasp the insights of the Reformation and the Augsburg Confession. Neither does he see the previously mentioned Fr. Jean Dez deal with this in his irenic book of 1688.

What are these 'new experiences?

> The teaching of the CA is that God 'imputes' the saving faith of the sinner, who has the satisfaction-making Christ transferred to himself in the consolation of the Word and in the reception of the holy sacraments. This faith, which includes Christ, God imputes pro justitia coram ipso ('for righteousness in his sight'). The total and personal righteousness of the obedient and atoning Christ . . . transforms the total sinner into a personal and total new

22. Lackmann, *Catholic Unity* Chapter 3.

man in possession of the ... intrinsic passive righteousness. Now a 'new creature' appears, moved by the active, living righteousness of the Spirit. This transforming, total, and personal character of the justifying event cannot be properly expressed with the help of the traditional scholastic formulas used by Dez (nor, for that matter, with the formulas of Trent). Here lies a new Catholic insight which must still be mastered 'in terms of a Catholic understanding.'[23]

Lackmann explains that such faith is obtained by the preaching of the Gospel and sacraments and that through these God gives us His Holy Spirit which helps us to relate *personally* to Christ as "reborn Children of God". Through the Word of preaching the Gospel, and then through absolution and the sacrament of repentance (that is separate from the sacrament of the Altar), "God gives new life and comfort of the heart".[24]

**Rev. Max Lackmann's Prison Record in Dachau Concentration Camp**

23. Lackmann, *Catholic Unity*. 79
24. Lackmann, *Catholic Unity*.81

## Una Sancta

Lackmann calls on the Church by saying that preaching itself has the presence of God, which is different from his bodily presence in the Sacrament of the Altar: it is not to be thought of as dogmatic and moral instruction *about* salvation. The preaching of the Word of God itself is "holy ground"—a jewel in the Church, and a holy treasure *apart from* the sacrament of the Altar at Mass. To Lackmann, this idea—for his perception of the church *before* the Vatican Council at least, if not for today,—is a "completely foreign notion".[25] He goes on to say "One misses every consideration of the New Testament idea—so important in the Augsburg Confession—that the proclamation of the 'Kingdom of God' in the Gospel is a most important ingredient of worship, that it belongs, together with the Liturgy and the celebration of the Sacrament in the continuous 'sacrifice of praise' of the regular mass."[26] Lackmann also sees an insight that was taken up in Vatican 2: he says the "divine dignity "of the priesthood is also demonstrated that it is a *preaching* ministry: it is not limited to a ministry of prayer to God at the altar. He says "there is also a priestly ministry directed to people in the dispensing of absolution and the Word."[27] Lackmann disputes the idea of Fr. Dez that the authority to consecrate the elements *alone* "is the heart and core of the priestly office."[28] Christ, to Lackmann, is also present in the ministry of preaching or what we might call today 'evangelization'. In the Augsburg Confession, the preaching of the Gospel awakens faith and brings about repentance and the total life-long conversion of the Christian until final death in the discarding of the 'old man' and the new birth in Christ.[29] These teachings were meant to be "part of the faith of the Mother Church, renewing and complementing the existing faith and life of the Church."[30] Lackmann tellingly asks which of these beliefs and ideas can

---

25. Lackmann, *Catholic Unity* 81

26. Lackmann, *Catholic Unity*, 82

27. Fr Kenan Osborne in his Book "A History of the ordained ministry in the Roman Catholic Church' states' in the document '*De Sacerdotibus*' the preparatory document for Priesthood for Vatican II ( June 1960) the Bishops clearly desired at the beginning of the document the threefold ministry of Jesus i.e. teacher, priest and pastor be mentioned and in the threefold designation of ministries the first to be named was that of teacher i.e. the ministry of preaching the Word. Osborne Kenan Priesthood O.F.M '*A History of the Ordained Ministry in the Roman Catholic Church*' Paulist Press NY 1988 p. 309–10

28. Lackmann, *Catholic unity*, 83 (author's italics on '*alone*')

29. Lackmann, *Catholic Unity*, 83

30. Lackmann, *Catholic Unity*. 84

truly be characterized as 'Protestant perversions' with a good churchly and theological conscience?[31]

According to Lackmann, a copy of the original Augsburg Confession in German was available to the Council Fathers at Trent, but the points and 'gifts' of the Confession were not accepted and heeded; rather the Fathers— to Lackmann- 'defended the old' and 'excluded the new'. However at the time of writing his book he sees a new openness in Catholicism to these notions, ideas and beliefs, and with this, a deeper listening to the heart of the Gospel's call to deeper conversion to Christ and feels that "then doors will very soon open which have been locked until now."[32] It is interesting to reflect on Lackmann's theses in this period after the Council. Did the doors indeed continue to open? One might digress at this time to consider:

Pope Saint John XXIII prayed for a new Pentecost for the church, renewing the ancient gifts of the Spirit as experienced in the Day of Pentecost.[33] The prayer was indeed answered in, amongst others, the Charismatic renewal movement of the 60's and 70's. The question might have been asked at the time whether *that* move of the Holy Spirit would be accepted or rejected by the church as 'being' (or not being)—in line with Catholic orthodoxy and doctrine. Like the Reformation, the movement too was inspired from the peripheries of Christendom, from outside the bounds of the Catholic church itself, from the Pentecostal Christian stream in America, far from Rome's orthodoxies.

God saw that the Church did in fact 'open the doors to the Redeemer', and on several occasions St Peter's itself was filled with the sounds of singing in tongues, and Catholics worshipping God with outstretched arms in the presence of the Popes. Pope Paul VI spoke of the renewal as "an opportunity for the Church" and Pope Saint John Paul II spoke of it as a "new springtime" brought forth by the Spirit.[34] Pope Francis in an address

---

31. Lackmann, *Catholic Unity*, 84

32. Lackmann, *Catholic Unity*, 85

33. Prayer of Pope Saint John XXIII for a new Pentecost "Renew, Your wonders in this our day, as by a new Pentecost. Grant to Your Church that, being of one mind and steadfast in prayer with Mary, the Mother of Jesus, and following the lead of blessed Peter, it may advance the reign of our Divine Savior, the reign of truth and justice, the reign of love and peace. Amen" Come, Holy Spirit, in your power and might to renew the face of the earth. https://www.pentecosttodayusa.org/wp-content/uploads/2022/02/Burning-Bush-Novena2015.pdf

34. https://www.vatican.va/jubilee_2000/magazine/documents/ju_mag_01061998_p-04_en.html

to the Leaders of the international Catholic Charismatic renewal in 2019 encouraged the assembly "- to share baptism in the Holy Spirit with everyone in the Church. It is the grace you have received. Share it! Don't keep it to yourselves!—to serve the unity of the body of Christ, the Church, the community of believers in Jesus Christ".[35] One wonders what Luther himself and Melanchthon and indeed Asmussen and Lackmann would have thought of this evangelical endorsement? What is impossible for man, God can do; what was impossible at Augsburg, God has been doing across the world in these last decades in the heart of the Church.

We revert to Lackmann's remaining theses:

In the fifth theses Lackmann refers to abuses in the Church which he regards as 'anti-Catholic' and 'anti-Roman', which the Church itself needed to address. The AC asks for clarity on a wide range of issues—such as the question of Justification, the role of good works, the question of communion under both kinds, the Mass itself and the vows of Monastics. In this light, Lackmann asks for Catholics to understand the Reformed viewpoint: with what they see as abuses he wishes to remind the Church that 'anti-Roman' and 'anti-Catholic negatives 'were expressed by Christians who desired the 'peace of the City' and who had neither 'enthusiasm nor joy' for the frightful disunity within Mother Church.

> They said sharp things against the Church; but they did so because they struggled and suffered for something which the Universal Catholic Church dared not lack. What this 'something' is must be made clear also in their negatives.[36]

The Reformers were seeking clarity on a whole range of issues and abuses: they were unafraid to spell them out, perhaps in the same way as people today have criticized the church for its failure to deal with abuse, or its lack of clarity over issues of faith, practice or doctrine. Finally, Lackmann deals with the dissolution that happened to the church in the wake of the failure to agree at Augsburg. The breakup was contrary to the many scriptural premises encouraging unity and humility, such as 1 Corinthians 1:10, and thus was itself 'non-Catholic'.

---

35. Address of Pope Francis to participants in the international conference of Leaders of the Catholic Charismatic Renewal international Service Charis June 8, 2019, https://www.vatican.va/content/francesco/en/speeches/2019/june/documents/papa-francesco_20190608_charis.pdf

36. Lackmann, Catholic Unity, 107

> Now I beseech you, brethren, through the name of our Lord Jesus Christ, that ye all speak the same thing and that there be no divisions among you; but that ye be perfected together in the same mind and in the same judgment.[37]

As recent Popes and Bishops have stated the failure to agree at Augsburg was the fault of both sides; today it is no longer possible to blame one side or the other. Pope Saint John Paul II, on the occasion of the 500th anniversary of the birth of Martin Luther in 1983, gave a speech in German in the Lutheran Church in Rome. The New York times reported the Pope as saying—

> Roman Catholic and Protestant studies have yielded a more balanced picture of Luther's personality and the realities of the 16th century, [the Pope continued] and shown that "the rupture in ecclesiastical unity cannot be reduced to the lack of comprehension by Catholic Church authorities or solely to Luther's lack of understanding of true Catholicism, even if both factors played a role." The Pope called for continued historical research, "that does not take sides, motivated only be the search for truth," to provide "a true image' of Luther and the Reformation. 'Guilt, wherever it exists, must be recognized, on whichever side it is found.'[38]

Lackmann asks "How did the Catholicity which both sides endeavored to represent result in an uncatholic stance because of their opposition to one another?[39] An unfortunate element of pride seemed to damage both sides. Melanchthon described the Fathers of Trent as

> unlearned [who know] about as much of divine doctrine as the asses on which they ride, since they have heathen and un-Christian teaching and Church. And because they serve their bellies, seeking and seeing only the voluptuous pleasures of this life, so that our teaching makes them uneasy, they are bitterly hostile to us.[40]

Lackmann remarks that such words are unjustified and inappropriate "in view of the theological and ecclesiastical accomplishments of the Council". On the other hand, the Catholic Church has only recently accepted

---

37. https://bible.knowing-jesus.com/topics/Agreeing-With-One-Another/type/asv 1 Corinthians 1:10

38. https://www.nytimes.com/1983/11/06/world/pope-praises-luther-in-an-appeal-for-unity-on-protest-anniversary.html

39. Lackmann, *Catholic Unity*, 108

40. Lackmann, *Catholic Unity*, 109

its part in the breakup of Western Christianity. As late as the early 20th century, it used *similar* language to describe the work of the Reformers in official documents. Lackmann quotes from an encyclical written by Pope Pius X—issued on May 26th 1910—called '*Editae seape*':

> There arose proud and rebellious men, enemies of the cross of Christ, men with a worldly mentality, whose god was their belly, who did not strive for the improvement of morality, but rather for the denial of the most important teachings of the faith. They threw everything into confusion and prepared for themselves and for others a broad pathway to licentious autocracy; or else they sought openly, by means of contempt for ecclesiastical authority and leadership, according to the whims of the most degenerate princes and peoples, violently to destroy the Church's doctrine, constitution, and discipline.[41]

It would seem that both sides have broken apart that which belonged together in one church. Each side to Lackmann presented its Catholic substance in a 'questionable Catholic form';[42] such an attitude resulted in both the Reformers and the Curia unable to understand each other, or even to try to do so. The Reformers viewed what they saw of the 'horizontal' (which Lackmann lists as papacy, Bishops, priests, Canon Law, Mass, Liturgy and practice, pious works, penance etc.)[43] as essentially denying the Gospel and the saving work of Christ. They saw that the 'humanity of Christ'—that which had been taken up into fellowship with Christ—had been lost, with the Church no longer mediating the saving work of the Gospel in the world, making the Church seem like "a new form of Judaism", without the promised Spirit-filled life of Pentecost. The Church that the Reformers viewed seem to seek salvation by a constant striving by personal willpower to reach heaven, placing the work of the Gospel in almost opposition to a semi-Pelagianism of good works. Lackmann challenged this presupposition and asked why the Reformers brought their message in a way which deprecated the ancient church and its practices, preserving instead of breaking down the churchly institutions and traditions? Both sides were defending Catholic truths in an "un-Catholic fashion." True Christian insight, however, is demonstrated by an integration into the previous existing whole, understanding its own gift as proceeding from the deposit

---

41. Lackmann, *Catholic Unity*,109
42. Lackmann, *Catholic Unity*,110
43. Lackmann, *Catholic Unity*129

given in the New Testament, the Liturgy, Dogma and Theology. Lackmann illustrates his theses with a metaphor:

> [The new spiritual insight] is a building stone in the already existing building: in order to be this, it must allow its corners and dimensions to be shaped to fit. If it finds no place in the great structure, the insight and not the whole building must yield.[44]

The danger comprises trying to make the whole yield to the new insight or movement. Lackmann says that Luther often spoke of 'his gospel', which he then used as a standard by which to judge whether any Church father was useful, or "even whether a statement of scripture was binding for faith".[45] Basing everything on personal experience can mean that no theological or moral obligation need be considered or obeyed. This is where Lackman places the failure of the Augsburg process as the Reformers were no longer basing themselves on the foundations of the Church—the 'pillar' and ground of truth. (1 Timothy 3:14–15). Instead, they ended with Evangelical principles and teaching on the Lord's support, justification, ministry, sacraments and Church, separated from Roman Catholic pre-suppositions and "the previously given Western experiences of faith and Church." Lackmann feels that such a path as diverted, and the longer it exists in isolation, the more it turns on itself and decomposes. Instead of being a corrective, it has lost the object for which it should offer a corrective, and thus "loses the reason for its existence." Sadly, Lackmann concludes, in losing the sight of Catholic Christianity in East and West, all that remains is. . .Protestantism.[46] On the other hand, Lackmann sees the dry scholasticism in the Church of that time where there was very little to distinguish an honorable heathen from a Christian one: Reason ruled over Revelation, and so the Church was not in a position to understand what the Reformers wanted. Lackman summarizes his theses and his work on The Augsburg Confession and Catholic unity:

---

44. Lackmann, *Catholic Unity*, 133

45. Lackmann, *Catholic Unity*, 135 Luther wrote: "We should throw the epistle of James out of this school, for it doesn't amount to much. It contains not a syllable about Christ. Not once does it mention Christ, except at the beginning. I maintain that some Jew wrote it who probably heard about Christian people but never encountered any. Since he heard that Christians place great weight on faith in Christ, he thought, 'Wait a moment! I'll oppose them and urge works alone'. https://zondervanacademic.com/blog/martin-luther-james-bible

46. Lackmann, *Catholic Unity*, 139

> If one takes the *Confutatio Pontificia* and its echo, Melanchthon's *Apology*, it is very difficult to avoid the conclusion: there was at that time no alternative to schism. But this was not a Catholic solution, either from the standpoint of the confessors of Augsburg or from the standpoint of the curia. The Church did not complete the task to which it was called. Its completion has been simply delayed. Neither Peace of Augsburg nor the Council of Trent completed the task.[47]

He pleads for Catholics and Lutherans to take a fresh look at the Document that caused their division—the Augsburg Confession—and to bring the work of the Diet of Augsburg to its real conclusion: a renewed vital united evangelical Catholic Church.

The task is not yet accomplished.

He concludes:

> I would like to assume that this volume has demonstrated how the *Confessio Augustana* draws separated Christians into an intensive movement toward each other. The CA will release great forces of truth, love, return, humility, hope, if we attempt to bring the difficult historical struggle of those decades into the presence of the Lord of the Church. We should not fear such a movement toward one another. The CA is a sign placed by God to remind us that Evangelical and Catholic Christians cannot escape each other, that the Reformation still awaits its fulfillment in a manner which will bring Evangelicals and Catholics together into one Church: Not at the expense of the truth, but through the truth. For the truth alone will make both parts of Western Christendom free for one another. The service which the Augsburg confession can perform in this work of Christ (i.e, our being made free for one another) certainly still lies before us. The CA is anything but a dusty document of history. 'History is living,' wrote Karl August Meissinger in his little volume. Luther, die deutsche Tragödie, 1521; 'it would be dead if it did not always touch off new impulses. It always comes to life if these new impulses are seized and used.'[48]

Max Lackmann spent much of his latter years giving ecumenical Bible retreats in a Center now called the Hans Asmussen House in Gersfeld-Dalherda, near Fulda. It is not known how he may have reacted to the Joint Declaration on the Doctrine of Justification which he actually lived

---

47. Lackmann, *Catholic Unity*, 141–42
48. Lackmann, *Catholic Unity*, 142

to see. He died on January 11, 2000 and is buried with his wife Elsa Maria Lackmann in a graveyard in Fulda. Max Lackmann said, "one is either a Catholic Christian or one is no Christian."[49] He was 'pensioned off' early for his 'Catholic tendencies'. As if to rebuff this accusation, he wrote:

> We say—Yes to tradition and no to traditionalism, yes to the office of the Pope, and no to papalism. Yes, to the canon of the Church, no to legalism. To Mary the most blessed Mother of God we say yes! But we must say no to Marianism! Yes, to the institution of the Church and to episcopacy, confession etc., but no to institutionalism. Yes, to the abundant grace of the holy sacraments and to the sacramental character of the Church: no to sacramentalism. Yes, to Rome as the central See, but no to centralism and Romanism.[50]

His colleague in Die Sammlung, Hans Asmussen, was the provost of Kiel from 1948 until 1955. He later retired to Heidelberg where he continued to write and lecture. His dedication to ecumenism brought him many enemies, who accused him of having 'catholic tendencies'. He died on the 30th of December 1968 and was buried in Kiel. His inscription read "auf das sie alle eines seien,"—that they may all be one (John 17:21).[51] It was the same text that had been placed on the grave of his friend Cardinal Bea who had died the previous month on November 16th, 1968 and who was buried in his native Riedböhringen, in Baden-Württemberg.[52]

---

49. Asmussen Ed *The Unfinished Reformation,*.106
50. Asmussen Ed *The Unfinished Reformation,*.106
51. https://en.evangelischer-widerstand.de/html/view.php?type=dokument&id=206&l=
52. Stjepan Schmidt Augustin Bea New City Press New York 1992 p.714

# 11

# Blessed Max Joseph Metzger (1887–1944) and the Una Sancta Movement

## PEACE WORK

Dr Max Josef Metzger, founder of the *Una Sancta Brotherhood* and ecumenical movement was born in Schopfheim in the Black Forest on February 3rd, 1887. Ordained as a priest in 1911, he was a man of great vision and courage and might be described today as a type of religious 'entrepreneur'—always turning his mind to new and needy areas and seeing how he could evoke a response from the faithful or from authorities to meet these perceived needs. According to Leonard Swidler, he "was never a person who could be satisfied with operating on a limited scale; he always attempted to draw ultimate conclusions and organize things on a world-wide basis.[1]" In succession, he turned his interests to the needs of alcoholics, operating alcohol-free restaurants, then running homes for the aged, epileptics, convalescents and young working girls.[2] After his own experience as a Chaplain in World War One he turned his thoughts to world peace and helped to found the *Weltfriedensbund der Weiße Kreuz*[3], co-operating

---

1. Swidler. *The Ecumenical Vanguard*,144–45
2. Swidler. *The Ecumenical Vanguard*, 145
3. The World Peace League of the White Cross. The 'White Cross' is the symbol on the Communion wafer.

with the *International Fellowship of Reconciliation (IFOR)*. Later, moving to the town of Meitingen, near Augsburg, in 1938, he opened a center for alcoholics and founded another society of men and women, married and single, called the *Gesellschaft Christi des Königs*.[4] This community was dedicated to performing pastoral and spiritual works of mercy, and to work for world peace and Christian unity. It was not long in these pre-war times that his mission got him in trouble with the Nazi Government, and he experienced several periods of imprisonment. Even when his hands and feet were bound in chains, he experienced a great desire to sing to relieve his feelings. He wrote:

> In spite of loneliness I am not bored. I study, read and write: I compose music and write poems, even if the music can't all be put down on paper…I have written three People's Masses in German, one of which I have sent to you"[5]

**Blessed Max Josef Metzger as a Division War Chaplain in World War 1914–1915.**

4. The Society of Christ the King.
5. Swidler, *The Ecumenical Vanguard*, 148–49

## Una Sancta

A turning point in his life came after attending the (non-Catholic) *World Conference of Faith and Order* in Lausanne with the status of Catholic 'observer'. Upon his return, and with the inspiration of his ecumenical experience in Switzerland, he decided to create a new organization called the *Una Sancta Brotherhood*. The aim of this group was to help create better Catholic-Lutheran relations. Although ecumenism was not new in Germany, his organization seemed to have a way to accelerate these efforts, giving them more structure, vision, and forward motion. Travelling throughout Germany and, making use of all his previous contacts, he sought to set up inter-confessional groups in all its major cities. The purpose of *Una Sancta* was thus to "serve rapprochement and mutual understanding between Christians of different confessions, in view of the last words of the Common Lord, 'That they may be one'".[6]

This might have involved simple fellowship meetings between local denominational clergy, or a lecture series in a neutral location, covering all areas of Christian doctrine. These gatherings were not to be open to all, to avoid polemics or possible argumentation. Thirdly, he envisaged discussion groups of mature people of different confessions, where there would be two different talks on a given topic given by speakers of different confessions, followed by free discussions by all. These meetings would open and close with common prayer or scripture, or prayers such as the Apostles Creed or the Our Father. In addition, because of the adverse political climate, everything had to be done to avoid suspicion by the police. Metzger's hope was that such meetings would help different Christians to see how much they held in common, and that apparent doctrinal contradictions were more due to different terminologies and linguistic expressions rather than 'deep-seated' or fundamental differences in belief. To encourage this 're-union' of Catholics and evangelicals, he wrote in his newspaper in 1934:

> Catholic brothers in faith, become evangelical! Not that you should leave the Catholic Church, but that you should fulfill its real and ultimate calling. Evangelical renewal, a thorough Christianization of the Church is the essential prerequisite, so that the serious Christian of the Evangelical Church may recognize that here is Christ and his Gospel pure and unfalsified, in full unbroken vital power. Evangelical' brothers, become Catholic! Free yourselves from negative protestation, from pre-judgement, from all narrowness of national and racist attachment! Take up again where your forefathers left off! Make their demands you own—the genuine

6. Swidler, *The Ecumenical Vanguard*, 150

evangelical renewal of the Church. It will not be accomplished by holding oneself aloof from the life springs of the Church, but rather by living from them and by working together with all earnestly striving Christians to build up the communion of saints, in the one, holy, catholic and apostolic church.

Catholics become evangelical! Evangelicals become Catholic!

Then there will be the *Una Sancta*, the one holy Church for which we jointly strive and pray.[7]

As a response to this favorable reaction to his appeal, Dr Metzger proceeded to organize annual conferences in his center in Meitingen,—the first taking place during Pentecost 1939 and the second in August 1940 on the subject of 'The Church'. Both were a success and described as being very 'harmonious', drawing numerous Lutheran clergy together with University Professors and Pastors from his own Society of Christ the King, Augustinians, Benedictines, Jesuits and Carmelites. The meetings, however, were hounded by the Gestapo who were making arrests across Germany. Dr Max Josef decided to move to Berlin and continue his work there.

## LETTER TO PIUS XII

Seeing the need to grow this ecumenical endeavor, he wrote to Pius XII, sharing that non-Catholics had remarked that a 'certain proud self-righteousness' prevented the church from acknowledging its faults and errors, making the non-Catholics feel the Church was not able to serve in humility, but rather only with authority and a thirst for power and an all "too human spirit of self-assertion".[8] He was suggesting the need for a new Church Council to face these and other issues, and, as a prelude, he suggested that groups of twelve outstanding Catholic theologians and twelve outstanding non-Catholics in various territories meet and then report to the Vatican on their findings with a view to preparing for such a General Council. He commented "Church history and world history alike will raise a memorial to that wearer of the triple crown who begins that work on a generous scale and to the one who may perhaps finish it later."[9]

---

7. Swidler, *Bloodwitness*, 71
8. Swidler, *The Ecumenical Vanguard*, 156
9. Swidler. *The Ecumenical Vanguard* 156–58

UNA SANCTA

# THE DEVELOPMENT OF PADERBORN AND UNA SANCTA

Dr. Metzger's words and actions were certainly prophetic of the times and inspiration for Vatican II. His ideas for colloquia between outstanding Catholic and Protestant speakers to meet and discuss areas of concern evoked a response in the work of the Diocese of Paderborn, and Catholic Archbishop Jaeger and Lutheran Bishop Stählin of Oldenburg. Together they held such annual meetings of outstanding speakers from both Churches, in the years from 1947 until 1959, just before the time of the Vatican Council. The results of the meetings were all relayed to the Church in Rome. Metzger's final arrest happened in 1943, and he was imprisoned in Prinz Albrecht Strasse and then in Moabit Prison in Berlin. At a mock trial he received the death sentence. When the Judge Freisler asked him what 'Una Sancta' was, Metzger sought to explain, "Christ has founded only one church"... At this time the Judge became enraged, interrupted and repeated the words like a mantra "Una Sancta... Una Sancta...Una Sancta...This is us and there is no other!". Saying Dr. Metzger needed to be executed, he exclaimed, "I have never until this moment in my career used the word 'eradicate', but I use it here. Such a plague boil must be eradicated."[10] When the sentence was declared, Dr. Max Josef felt he had been honored. Able to speak to one of his associates before being removed from the court room he said,

> Now it is over, I am at peace. I have offered my life to God for the peace of the world and the unity of the Church. If God accepts it, I will be glad; if he grants me a longer life, I shall also be thankful. As God wills.[11]

On the day of his execution a prison guard witnessing the scene said: "Never have I seen a man die like that."[12] When his co-workers in the Society heard that he had been executed, they sang a 'Te Deum'. Dr. Max Josef was buried in St Hedwig's Cemetery in Berlin, the celebrant declaring that "He lived and died for the peace of nations and the re-union of faith." Later his remains were brought back to be interred in his native Meitingen.

Through his death and the death of other martyrs for faith, both Catholic and non-Catholic, Una Sancta experienced extraordinary growth from 1945–1948. Now a broad mass of people were hungering for an end to the divisions of faith, caused in the wake of the Reformation. They wished

10. Swidler, *Bloodwitness*, 102
11. Swidler *Bloodwitness*, 103
12. Swidler, *Bloodwitness*, 118

to see a visible church, pure in faith and freed from all political concerns, overtones, and corruption. Despite opposition and various crises, it had realistically helped to create a common ground between the churches that had not existed prior to the war, nor indeed since the Reformation.

## POST WAR DEVELOPMENTS OF UNA SANCTA

After the great turbulence of the Second World War, the late 1940's was a time for picking up the shattered remains of post war Germany. Huge displacement of German refugees, particularly from the East, meant great demographic changes in areas that had previously remained nearly all Protestant or all Catholic since the time of the Reformation. As Swidler relates "the purely Catholic communities in Bavaria in 1910 numbered over 2300; after the Second World war this sank to 9. Where in 1910 there were 244 purely Protestant communities today [Swidler wrote in 1966] there are none."[13] Every area of Germany was required to take a quota of displaced persons without regard to their religious denomination. The displacement of populations, together with common wartime experiences in such places as concentration camps, prisoner of war camps and refugee centers, created a soil where possible religious reconciliation between different Christian Churches could also take place. In these circumstances, both Catholic and Protestant Churches lent buildings to each other for services, something that would have been unthinkable previously—a practice that continues even today in the joint use of church buildings.

## GROWTH OF UNA SANCTA TO A PEOPLE'S MOVEMENT

This period gave birth to an unprecedented growth of Una Sancta, which during the war had effectively been purely an underground movement, and very much subject to Gestapo surveillance. Martyrdom of Christian leaders, such as with the execution of Metzger, created a new 'seedbed for the church'. Matthias Laros, who was asked to take over the leadership of Una Sancta at Meitingen, wrote that, while the Brotherhood had worked previously in an isolated and less organized fashion, "there had arisen now in the broad masses of people . . . an elemental will toward a final . . . fruitful

---

13. Swidler, *The Ecumenical Vanguard*, 168

elimination of the division of faith."[14] The Una Sancta Brotherhood which Metzger had created survived the war, and over the period from 1945 to 1950, grew to where it was estimated there were as many as 10,000 active participants in the Movement.[15] Groups varied in size from 10 members to some numbering over 200; Berlin itself had several Una Sancta Circles. When an Una Sancta evening was announced in Berlin, with speeches being given by alternatively Catholic, Lutheran, Orthodox and Baptist speakers, the church (with a capacity of 2,500) was "filled to overflowing half an hour ahead of time."[16] Similar meetings attracting hundreds of people were held in Frankfurt and Munich. In the northern town of Eberswalde over a thousand crammed into the largest venue available for talks by Protestant, Catholic and Free Church speakers. Ecumenical weeks were organized where lectures were given by Protestant and Catholic theologians. These were especially popular throughout the Rhineland, where priests and pastors presented to each other courses of their own theologies, on such challenging subjects as Papal Infallibility and the Augsburg Confession.

## KARL ADAM AND THE REASSESSMENT OF LUTHER

In Stuttgart, the famed Catholic theologian and University Professor Karl Adam gave a series of lectures on "Una Sancta from the Catholic Viewpoint", over three nights from April 27–29, 1947, to overflowing crowds at the Lutheran Markuskirche. Sensing the zeitgeist of the post war period, he deduced "it cannot be doubted that at the present moment, under the shattering impact of two world wars, at least in the sense that the unreality of mere polemic is being abandoned, that Luther on the one hand and the papacy on the other are being seen in a clearer and more friendly light, and that real efforts are being made , by Christians everywhere, to being about, if not a unio fidei, [union of faith] at least a unio caritatis [union of heart]."[17] Adam then proceeded to describe Luther, not in the former way as an arch heretic, fallen monk or even psychotic, but rather a man of great brilliance and a sharp incisive mind, who was horrified by sham holiness. To Adam, if Luther had brought these gifts to the service of the church and remained a

---

14. Laros, Una Sancta—Rundbrief September 1946 quoted in Swidler, *The Ecumenical Vanguard*, 171

15. Edward Grüber , 'Im Zeichen' 215 in Swidler, *The Ecumenical Vanguard*, 175

16. Swidler, *The Ecumenical Vanguard*, 176

17. Adam , *Roots of the Reformation*, 7

faithful Catholic, "he would be forever our Great Reformer, our True Man of God, our teacher, and leader, comparable to Thomas Aquinas and Francis of Assisi. He would have been the greatest saint of our people, the re- founder of the Church in Germany, a second Boniface."[18] The lectures were repeated later in Karlsruhe and later published both in German and English. When the book was later published with the title *Una Sancta in Katholischer Sicht*, he dedicated the book to the memory of Fr Max Josef Metzger.[19]

## GUIDING PRINCIPLES OF UNA SANCTA

One particular meeting in the Benedictine Abbey of Niederaltaich helped to bring the whole movement into clear focus. At a joint Catholic Protestant retreat, held in August 1946, the participants came up with three defining principles for Una Sancta work:

- In the effort toward mutual understanding there must be preparedness to learn from one another to practice Christian love.
- In the striving towards Christian truth, it is necessary that the divisive points be clearly seen. A union must not result at the expense of truth.
- The actual Union is the Work of God. God, however, works in history. Great historical events, great common needs can become in the hands of God decisive means of his grace when the hour is ripe. We can and must already now prepare ourselves for such a working of God's grace by taking the first two steps and by a sincere prayer for unity.[20]

The Stuttgart Una Sancta Circle sponsored an Una Sancta conference at the Benedictine Abbey of Neresheim with many important Christian leaders attending, including Hans Asmussen, President of the Chancery of the Evangelical Church in Germany and a member of *Die Sammlung* together with Catholic University Professors from Tubingen University. At this conference, two lectures were given by a Catholic and a Protestant speaker in memory of Max Metzger, "founder and blood martyr of the Una Sancta Movement."[21]

---

18. Adam, *Roots of the Reformation*, 26
19. Tr. Una Sancta in the Catholic perspective *One and Holy* 1951
20. Swidler, *The Ecumenical Vanguard*, 180
21. Swidler, *The Ecumenical Vanguard*, 181

Una Sancta

## YOUTH GATHERINGS AND PUBLICATIONS

While many renowned Churchmen and theologians from different confessions continued the intense sharing that Una Sancta involved, much larger gatherings were held for youth. On October 27, 1946, between three and four thousand students gathered for an ecumenical celebration at the Berlin Olympic Stadium, as a public demonstration for all baptized youth. A similar demonstration took place by several thousand students at Cologne University.[22] From some quiet almost clandestine meetings in World War Germany, post war Una Sancta grew into a national movement, with a wide variety of gatherings, meetings, conferences, lectures and demonstrations for Christian Unity. According to Laros, who became the official leader of Una Sancta at the invitation of Sister Gertrudis after the death of Metzger, it was now a "people's movement." It had also developed its own publishing, with a wide variety of publishing houses now spread the word across Germany. Una Sancta headquarters in Meitingen produced their own Rundbrief (Newsletter). It was estimated that over 50,000 copies of this Circular were distributed nationwide sharing their ecumenical vision and latest developments.

## THE MUNICH EUCHARISTIC CONGRESS 1960

Una Sancta went through various phases until its work was recognized in the Vatican with the foundation of the Pontifical Council for Christian Unity and the first agreement since the Reformation between Catholics and Lutherans in the *Joint Declaration on the Doctrine of Justification*. This historic document was signed by representatives of both churches in Augsburg in 1999. One of the major achievements of Una Sancta, on the route to Vatican II and the declaration was its participation in the 1960 Eucharistic Congress in Munich. The Congress was the first major international event to take place in Germany since the end of the war, attracting over a million people to Munich and was described as "the Dress Rehearsal for Vatican II."[23]. It created a great new sense of optimism for those attending, giving hope to those who had recently experienced the horrors of war. Its greatest

---

22. Swidler, *The Ecumenical Vanguard*, 186

23. Christoph Renzikowski, "Generalprobe für das Zweite Vatikanische Konzil," Domradio (July 30, 2010), https://www.domradio.de/artikel/kirchlicher-kongress-war-1960-erstes-mega-event-nach-dem-krieg.

innovation was, perhaps, the welcome given to the Munich Una Sancta Circle. This was the first time ever since Eucharistic Congresses had been established in Lille in France in 1881 that the Congress had an ecumenical dimension. Lutheran Frère Roger of the Taizé Community highlighted the scandal of the separation of the Churches and made a deep-felt plea for Christian Unity. Professor Heinrich Fries stated that the call for ecumenism could be heard across the whole Church for the first time.[24] The ecumenical aspect had reverberations outside the Congress as all of Germany was seeking peace and security after the disruption and chaos of the war. Professor Hans Küng said in this regard:

> No peace among the nations without peace among the religions. No peace among the religions without dialogue between the religions. No dialogue between the religions without investigation of the foundation of the religions."[25]

Konrad Adenauer himself, now as the Chancellor of West Germany wrote an address for the opening, in addition to attending the Congress in person on the final day:

> In 1939, the disaster of the Second World War began in Germany. These wounds have not closed to this day. Europe—indeed, the whole world—is still suffering. In the wake of this war, materialistic atheism went on an offensive all over the world and has stood at the heart of the European Continent since 1945, even threatening its spiritual core... Since the end of the war, a new element in the political image on the German people has been the cooperation of the members of the two Christian denominations, the Catholic and the Protestant, in public life. It was almost a creative act, a departure from a paralysis that had lasted for centuries, when the Union of Catholic and Protestant Christians, who had to suffer together under National Socialist persecution, formed after the collapse... May the Eucharistic World Congress in Munich strengthen these forces, make them resilient and let them continue to radiate."[26]

---

24. From a description of the Congress given to the author by Gudrun Steineck, Vorsitzende of the Oekumenische Kreise in Hofheim, Bavaria

25. https://www.goodreads.com/quotes/157789-no-peace-among-the-nations-without-peace-among-the-religions, taken from https://www.goodreads.com/work/quotes/84111.

26. Bulletin of the Press and Information Office of the Federal Government No. 139 of July 29, 1960, https://www.konrad-adenauer.de/seite/29-juli-1960/, p. 1381.

Adenauer had been aware how helpful the work of Una Sancta had been in bringing together a joint Christian Democratic Union Party which had succeeded beyond expectations in taking the reins of Government, fostering Germany's industrial and economic recovery, and encouraging its collective moral and spiritual revival and international standing. Now the message of Una Sancta in turn was going to reach the heart of the Vatican.

Una Sancta Munich—a group of about 500 Christians from different Churches wrote to Cardinal Wendel, the organizer of the Congress, asking to be included in the event. The application was not straightforward, as such ecumenical participation in such an event was unprecedented. The Canon Lawyer from Munich University, Professor Karl Mörsdorf, objected to their inclusion after permission was initially given, but, with the help of some influential friends, permission was once again granted. The Una Sancta Group were initially going to be placed in the Bayern Halle, but the delay now meant that that location was no longer available. Instead, the group were given the use of the Auditorium Maximum and the Atrium of Munich University at Geschwister-Scholl-Platz, made famous in the war by the resistance work of Sophie and the White Rose non-violent resistance group. Una Sancta were able to welcome an estimated nine thousand participants to their talks and presentations in the Congress, which were given in every available place, corridor, stairs, floor, including the Auditorium itself. It was only with the use of some gentle persuasion that they managed to usher all two hundred bishops, who wished to attend the talks, to their reserved seating. On the program were talks by the Abott M.Heufelder, OSB of Niederaltaich Monastery, a prominent center of Una Sancta activity, who gave the opening and closing talks. Fr. Thomas Sartory, also from the Monastery, gave a presentation on the Last Supper, while Dr. Otto Karrer, a Jesuit priest who had at one time become a Lutheran, gave a talk on "Eucharistic Thought among Our separated Brethren." The Una Sancta Group in Meitingen, where the Una Sancta movement was founded by Fr Metzger, gave a presentation on their work. When the Congress was over, Lutheran Bishop Wilhelm Stählin described the whole experience as a "world event". The Una Sancta Group prepared a special booklet to be distributed amongst all visitors, with articles by a wide variety of Christian authors and speakers from different backgrounds. All 8,000 copies were distributed, and for the three years following copies were reprinted until the organizers said "there was only one remaining copy". The move towards Church unity now seemed to be unstoppable even though many mountains had to be climbed but the doors were now open to the spiritual healing of wounds that had been received in the long years of separation. Later, in 2008 the Dublin Eucharistic Congress acknowledged the effect of the Munich Congress on ecumenism, where they stated:

> The first thirty-seven International Eucharistic Congresses did not deal with the themes of ecumenism and interreligious dialogue, except at the Congress of Jerusalem in 1893—although only partially and in a manner quite different from our approach today. The time had not yet come, but we can hope that coming years will see a greater openness to the essential link between the Eucharist and the communion of the Churches. If by its very nature the Eucharist manifests and realizes the *forma ecclesiae*, it represents not only the goal, but also the way and means of attaining visible communion between the Christian Churches. It was at Munich in 1960 that ecumenical relations began to take on their full importance at Eucharistic Congresses. Hardly had the preparations for the Second Vatican Council began when Blessed John XXIII decided to establish the Secretariat for the Promotion of Christian Unity. From then on, in the ecclesial context of Vatican II the movement towards Christian unity became part of the agenda of Eucharistic Congresses. This was followed in more recent times by interreligious dialogue, which has received such great attention in the Church since the first meeting at Assisi called by Pope John Paul II in 1986.'[27]

The influence of the Munich Congress carried over to the Second Vatican Council, the foundation of the Secretariate for Christian Unity, and subsequently the Pontifical Council for Christian Unity. This heralded the historic agreement on justification with the signing of the *Joint Declaration on the Doctrine of Justification in* Augsburg in 1999. Pope John Paul II stated in his encyclical, *Ut Unum Sint*, "It is absolutely clear that ecumenism, the movement promoting Christian unity, is not just some sort of appendix which is added to the Church's traditional activity. Rather, ecumenism is an organic part of her life and work and consequently must pervade all that she is and does."[28]

---

27. https://www.catholicculture.org/culture/library/view.cfm?recnum=9980

28. Pope Saint John Paul II, "Ut Unum Sint: On Commitment to Ecumenism," https://www.vatican.va/content/john-paul-ii/en/encyclicals/documents/hf_jp-ii_enc_25051995_ut-unum-sint.html, par 20.

# 12

# The Tide Begins to Turn

## JAEGER AND THE SECRETARIATE FOR CHRISTIAN UNITY

WE HAVE CHARTED SOME of the tides and cross currents of the Una Sancta Brotherhood and movement of Fr Max Josef Metzger, and the work of the Sammlung Group of Lutherans. These were movements of lay and ordained, who were seeking to create bonds of fellowship between divided Christians. Some of these eddies were beginning to reach the shores of the churches as a whole, and a slow growth of movement to Christian unity started to become visible. It was cautious at first, with a large measure of reserve. It seemed that the Holy Spirit was gently guiding church bodies towards unity. Once the general principle was elucidated—in the light of Jesus's own prayer for Christian Unity in John Chapter 17" that they may be one"—more formal and sometime 'hair-splitting' church-based agreements started to evolve, aided by the work of skilled, highly trained theologians. It involved many years and great effort to try to create a clear, welcoming path for the incoming tide of the Holy Spirit.

On the Protestant side, one can trace the role of ecumenism in the Edinburgh World Missionary Conference of 1910 and the World Conference of Faith and Order, which met in Lausanne, Switzerland in 1927. Attending this Swiss conference was the aforementioned Fr. Max Josef Metzger, the founder of the Una Sancta Brotherhood. This Conference came together

## The Tide Begins to Turn

with the Swedish 'Life and Work' and Swiss 'Faith and Order' in 1948 to form the World Council of Churches. The Lutheran World Federation which was founded in 1947 in Lund, Sweden, and was a part of the WCC, declared in 1948:

> In recognizing . . .these diversities as expressions of the one true apostolic faith and one Catholic Church, traditions have changed, antagonisms overcome, and mutual condemnations lifted. The diversities are reconciled and transformed into a legitimate and indispensable multiformity within the one body of Christ.[1]

The biggest development by far, in closing the gap between Catholic and Lutheran, was the advent of the Second Vatican Council (11 October 1962—8 December 1965). Before this, there had been a slow awakening of a new rebuilding of Church unity. One small- but important, step- happened on May 30th, 1960. Less than two years after becoming Pope, John XXIII invited his Cardinals to his private Library, where he announced the setting up of preparatory Commissions for what would become the Second Vatican Council.

> We have also in mind a special secretariate which will make it possible for separated brethren to follow the work of the Council, and thus to make easier their reunion in the one-fold of Christ. This will demonstrate the love of the Holy Father and his good will towards those who are called Christians, but who are separated from this Apostolic See.[2]

One month later on June 5th, 1960, the Pope further declared that he had set up what was to be known as the *Pontifical Secretariate for Christian Unity*, under the direction of German Cardinal Augustin Bea (1881–1968). Together with other Commissions, they would help prepare for the Council. This move was widely accepted by other Christian bodies, including the World Council of Churches at their meeting in St. Andrews in Scotland on the following month.

> The fact that a dialogue with the Roman Catholic Church now becomes possible is to be welcomed. The opportunity of a dialogue is welcome, but it means that the real difficulties are bound to come

---

1. Wood and Wengert, *Shared spiritual journey*, 36–37 There were some similar Lutheran bodies before the LWC as Professor Kolb related to the author: the Lutheran World Convention founded in 1923 and at least in Germany there was a similar organization in the nineteenth century.

2. Bea, *The Unity of Christians*, 50 Quoting Acta et doc 1, 95–98

> to the fore.... The World Council will profit by the opportunities which present themselves to make known to the new Secretariat the basic convictions and concerns of the World Council of Churches (for example, on religious liberty and on Christian social action, etc.).³

The Lutheran reaction from Hans Asmussen, member of the *Sammlung*, was also encouraging, seeing the Secretariate as promoting authentic dialogue between Lutheran and Catholic communities on the basis of truth: "The great possibility that Rome and Wittenberg may meet peacefully on the occasion of the Council must not be destroyed by unlawful compromise."

The President of the German Evangelical Federation, Professor Bornkamm, stated that: "the way to unity must require from no one the sacrifice of convictions imposed by conscience, and that doctrinal differences must not be set aside at the expense of truth."⁴

The Pontifical Secretariate had deep roots in the ecumenical movements in Germany. Following the martyrdom of Fr. Max Josef Metzger, his ecumenical work was taken up by Archbishop Jaeger of the Diocese of Paderborn. According to Jerome Michael Vereb, Archbishop Jaeger did not appreciate the personality of Metzger, but he suggested, as the proverb says "imitation renders consent": while not convinced of the man, he was however convinced of the cause.⁵ When the war was over, Jaeger established his own 'Una Sancta' meetings in his Diocese with the help of Lutheran Bishop Wilhelm Stählin. Again, using the same 'Metzger' title of 'Una Sancta', he established his first ecumenical study group of Protestant and Catholic theologians on 2/3 April 1946. Swidler in his book *The Ecumenical Vanguard* describes this high level of theological discourse as follows.

> Once each year the Catholics invited the Protestants to Paderborn for a conference; for a second semi-annual conference the Protestants were the hosts. The conferences always began on a Monday and ran to Friday; the participants lived, ate and worked together. Usually about four lectures were delivered on previously selected themes, and much time was given over to open, often very energetic, discussion. The personnel of the conferences have remained almost constant, about twelve theologians and one or

---

3. Bea, *The Unity of Christians*, 135
4. Bea, *The Unity of Christians*, 138
5. Vereb *Because he was a German*, 105

two non-theologians from each side; no one new may be invited without the approval of both sides. The subjects of the conferences have been of the most profound and often controversial sort, such as death, immortality, faith and works, and Mary. When differences of opinion arise, the spirit is not always Catholic versus Protestant; it sometimes cuts across both sides. The meetings have taken place regularly without fail, even during the troubled years between 1948 and 1951, although since about 1957 they have been cut down to one a year at the request of the Protestant members, who felt themselves pressed with so much other demanding work. When asked in 1959 what results he thought he could see in the thirteen years of meeting, Bishop Stählin said that the opinion and understanding both sides have of each other have vastly improved; today's situation would have been considered absolutely impossible a few years ago.[6]

With this long experience of ecumenical dialog and fellowship, on March 4th 1960 Jaeger wrote a letter of petition of Pope John XXIII, asking for a permanent (Una Sancta—type) office in the Roman Curia "to promote the cause of Christian Unity, to alleviate prejudice within the Christian family, and to facilitate ready access to clear and precise information, for the sake of a non- Catholic constituency ". He wrote:

> Most Holy Father: Humbly prostrate at the feet of Your Holiness, I, the Archbishop of Paderborn, and the President of the Institute named after Johann Adam Möhler, together with the Vice Rector and the directors of the Institute, eagerly request Your Holiness to deign to establish a Pontifical Commission to Promote Christian Unity. The role of this Commission would be to observe and to help those meetings and projects, which would unite all those who were baptized, and believe in Christ the Lord into One, Holy, Catholic, and Apostolic Roman Church. Such a Commission, founded and directed by the Apostolic See, would be of great importance in fostering and promoting that inclination toward the Apostolic See, which, under the inspiration of the Holy Spirit has already risen up in many countries and which has overcome and rooted out many false, prejudicial opinions in the search for truth, as Your Holiness so clearly explained in your encyclical *Ad Petri Cathedram*.[7]

---

6. Swidler, *The Ecumenical Vanguard* 199–200
Swidler notes that among those participating in these conferences were Wilhelm Stählin, Hans Asmussen, Wolfhart Pannenberg, Lorenz Jaeger, Josef Lortz, and Karl Rahner,

7. Vereb. *Because he was a German*,184

Jaeger's request found its echo and response in the Pontificate of Pope John. The person chosen to lead the new Secretariate, Cardinal Augustin Bea S.J., was also, like Jaeger, a German, Jesuit who was, at this time, the Rector and Professor of the Pontifical Bible institute in Rome. Not alone was his background in the war situation in Germany and Italy (where he had harbored Jewish refugees) but he had received his training in Philology, Archeology and Hermeneutics in Berlin, and not in a Roman Pontifical Institute. His teachers were both Protestant and German, helping to infuse his own ecumenical Biblical aptitudes. Bea was quickly nominated as the first President of the *Pontifical Institute for Christian Unity*, an Institute or Department which had never existed previously within the Vatican. When asked why Bea was nominated to this position, Archbishop Lorenz Caprovilla, the Private Secretary to Pope John, said simply "because he was a German."[8] In every way—academically, historically, ethnically and personally- he was ideally suited to such work.

The Pope himself had nurtured a deep commitment to Christian unity. He wanted the call to unity to be a central element in the Church Council he wished to inaugurate. In *Ad Petri Cathedram,*—the first encyclical he wrote as Pope—he quoted the famous words of Saint Augustine:

> Allow us to express our affection for you and to call you the legacy of our sons and brothers . . . We address you, then, as brothers even though you are separated from us. For as St Augustine said: "Whether they like it or not, they are our brothers. They will only cease to be our brothers when they cease to say: Our Father."[9]

Bea himself was quick to recognize that the schism of the Western Church was now over 400 years old; generations had grown up in different parts of the body of Christ, who wished to remain loyal to the legacy they had received during this time. Whilst Catholics wished to remain loyal to their Church backgrounds, so did Lutherans, Anglicans, and others. This created extra challenges for reunion:

> The historical fact is too complicated to be the object of human judgement: God alone can unravel the threads of that tangled skein of history. And when we look at the individual situation of our separated brethren, we find that the vast majority only accept the legacy handed down to them from their ancestors. Just as it is no merit of us Catholics that we were born in a family already

8. Vereb *Because he was a German,*3
9. Pope Saint John XXIII *Ad Petri Catherdram*, 86

belonging to the Catholic Church, so it is no fault of theirs to be sons of parents separated from our Church. And so, in accepting the legacy handed down to them, these non-Catholics, in good faith, are convinced that they are on the right path. So, when we speak of the obstacles to union, we do not wish to deny the deep longing for union that exists today among all classes of our separated brethren. This longing is certainly the work of the Holy Spirit, something to gladden all of us who are children of the Church and also to stimulate us to give our help to all those who sincerely seek the truth.[10]

Bea was also aware that the separation in some of these church divisions (and we might add here the Diet of Augsburg) were not of their choosing: He writes:

> Even in their separation they have kept, in varying degrees, much of the rich inheritance of truth and devotion which derives from the Mother Church, and indeed, in many cases they were originally cut off from this Church, not of their own choosing, but on account of the *absolute power of prince or the bad example of worldly prelate*. Those among them who hold faithfully to the doctrines inherited from their Catholic ancestors and try to live according to them, easily come to recognize that they do not possess the whole truth and that they lack many aids which our Lord has promised to his faithful.[11]

The Council went even beyond this position: they encouraged the Catholic faithful to learn, receive and treasure lessons and insights received by fellow Christians during the long years of separation, and not just wish to impart to others any wisdom gained from their own traditions.

## THE SECOND VATICAN COUNCIL 1962–65

In the formal announcement for the Council given during the annual week for Christian Unity in January 1959, Pope Saint John XXIII wanted to invite separated communities "to seek again that unity for which so many souls were longing in these days throughout the world." He said:

---

10. Bea *The Unity of Christians* 39–40

11. Bea *The Unity of Christians*,.42 italics are of the author. One would nearly think in this expression that Bea is directly describing the situation experienced at the Diet of Augsburg.

> To this chorus of prayers, we also invite all Christians of Churches separated from Rome, so that the Council may also be to their advantage. We know that many of these children are eager for a return of unity and peace, in accordance with the teaching and the prayer of Christ to the Father. And we know that the announcement of the Council was not only received by them with joy, but that more than a few of them have already promised to offer their prayers for its success and hope to send representatives of their communities to follow its work at close hand. All of this is for us a cause of great comfort and hope and it is precisely to facilitate these contacts that we established some time ago a Secretariat for this precise purpose."[12]

At the opening of the Council, the Pope went further in expressing his "deep sadness" at the "prolonged separation" of the communities of the non-Catholic observers and the Catholic Church, saying . "If we are in any way to blame for the separation, we humbly ask for forgiveness and pardon of our brethren who feel that have been injured by us."[13]

In addition, he added

> For our part we willingly forgive the injuries which the Catholic Church has suffered, and forget the grief endured during the long series of dissentions and separations. May the Heavenly Father deign to hear our prayers and true heavenly peace.[14]

This was a very different attitude and preamble to the Council of Trent. Even though they were invited, no 'non-Catholic' [Lutheran] observers were present for the duration of the Council, and the stated purpose of the Council had been to extirpate all heresy. This time, non-Catholics were present as observers from the beginning, (including, from our perspective, Lutheran pastor Rev. Max Lackmann). The Documents of the Council, too, had a different tone: gone were all anathemas, and the wording of the different declarations was irenic and open to non- Catholic response and consideration. In the opening document called the *Dogmatic Constitution of the Church (Lumen Gentium)*, the Council declared that "This Church

---

12. Pope Saint John XXIII *Humanae Salutis* December 25 1961 Convoking the Council for 1962

13. Wood and Wengert *Spiritual Journey*, 38

14. Wood and Wengert. *Spiritual Journey*, 38 With such a humble admission, it is perhaps then not surprising that Pope John XXIII is also commemorated in the Anglican Church of Canada and Evangelical Lutheran Churches in America each year on the 3 or 4 June. https://en.wikipedia.org/wiki/Pope_John_XXIII

constituted and organized in the world as a society, in the Catholic Church, which is governed by the successor of Peter and by the Bishops in communion with him, although many elements of sanctification and of truth are found outside of its visible structure. These elements, as gifts belonging to the Church of Christ, are forces impelling toward catholic unity."[15]

Previously, the encyclical of Pius XII *Mystici Corporis* (1943) was not so irenic: it simply identified the Church of Christ with the Catholic Church: the only way to church unity was for individuals to join the Catholic Church:

> They, therefore, walk in the path of dangerous error who believe that they can accept Christ as the Head of the Church, while not adhering loyally to His Vicar on earth. They have taken away the visible head, broken the visible bonds of unity and left the Mystical Body of the Redeemer so obscured and so maimed, that those who are seeking the haven of eternal salvation can neither see it nor find it. . . For even though by an unconscious desire and longing they have a certain relationship with the Mystical Body of the Redeemer, they still remain deprived of those many heavenly gifts and helps which can only be enjoyed in the Catholic Church. Therefore, may they enter into Catholic unity and, joined with Us in the one, organic Body of Jesus Christ, may they together with us run on to the one Head in the Society of glorious love. Persevering in prayer to the Spirit of love and truth, We wait for them with open and outstretched arms to come not to a stranger's house, but to their own, their Father's home.[16]

On the other hand, the Decree of Ecumenism, *Unitatis Redintegratio* (1964), moved the whole Vatican II discourse further in helping Christians from different churches to relate to each other. Before the Council, strict prohibitions had been in place to prevent any engagement between present day Catholics and non-Catholics. They were held as 'guilty' of not being part of the Church, even though the schism of 1530 was, in fact, none of their fault. In 1928, Pius XI had written in his letter *Mortalium Animos*, "it is clear why the apostolic see has never allowed its subjects to take part in Assemblies of non-Catholics: for the union of Christians can only be

---

15. Flannery, *Vatican II Documents* 'Lumen Gentium' 357

16. Vatican Documents *Pius XII Mystici Corporis* https://www.vatican.va/content/pius-xii/en/encyclicals/documents/hf_p-xii_enc_29061943_mystici-corporis-christi.html 41 & 91/177

promoted by promoting the return to the one True Church of Christ of those who are separated from it, for in the past they have unhappily left."[17]

In contrast, Vatican II Decree on Ecumenism stated

> Moreover some, and even most of the significant elements and endowments which together go to build up and give life to the church itself can exist outside the visible boundaries of the Catholic Church: the written Word of God; the life of Grace; faith hope and love with other interior gifts of the Holy Spirit and visible elements too.

The document continued:

> Our separated Brothers and Sisters also celebrate many sacred actions of the Christian religion. They most certainly can truly engender a life of grace...and just be held capable of giving access to that communion which is salvation...for the Spirit of Christ has not refrained them from using them as a means of salvation which derive their efficacy for the very fullness of grace and truth entrusted to the Catholic Church[18]

Even more striking, from our point of view and that of the Reformation impasse, it states:

> On the other hand, Catholics must gladly acknowledge and esteem the truly Christian endowments for our common heritage which are to be found among our separated brethren. It is right and salutary to recognize the riches of Christ and virtuous works in the lives of others who are bearing witness to Christ, sometimes even to the shedding of their blood. For God is always wonderful in his works and worthy of all praise. Nor should we forget that anything wrought by the grace of the Holy Spirit in the hearts of our separated brethren can contribute to our own edification. Whatever is truly Christian is never contrary to what genuinely belongs to the faith; indeed, it can always bring a more perfect realization of the very mystery of Christ and the Church.[19]

This beautiful piece is completely irenic; we could hardly compare it with what we have heard at the Augsburg Diet, which was full of recrimination, or of previous Councils since the Reformation. Such a declaration would have been unthinkable before Vatican II: the very idea that Catholics

17. Wood and Wengert, *Spiritual Journey*, 40
18. Flannery, *Vatican Documents* Unitatis Redintegratio.455
19. Flannery, Vatican Documents, Unitatis Redintegratio,458

might benefit and profit by their encounter with non-Catholics was regarded as practically impossible. Sharing together, on the other hand, as this passage suggests, makes us better Christians: Catholics, Anglicans, Lutherans and all. We are, according to this statement, gifts to each other—not enemies who would seek to fight each other or eliminate us by argument: if we belong to Christ, we belong to each other.

After the Council, the Decree on Ecumenism led to a plethora of other bridge-building works—a little like a renovation of an old building that had fallen badly into disrepair; the pieces were slowly being reassembled together to the Glory of God.

## THE PROBLEMS OF THE MUTUAL CONDEMNATIONS OF THE REFORMATION ERA

One key area in unraveling the knots created by the Reformation events has been the issue of mutual condemnations by both sides, after the Augsburg Diet. It was necessary to examine afresh the buried common ground of doctrine, as well as the rationale behind the mutual condemnations. A study was undertaken by Cardinal Karl Lehmann of Mainz (1936–2018) and Lutheran Theologian Wolfhart Pannenberg (1928–2014) for this purpose. The initiative came as a result of a visit of Pope Saint John Paul II to meet Protestant Christians in Mainz on 17th November 1980. Bishop Eduard Lohse of the United Evangelical Lutheran Church of Germany (VELKD) pleaded at that time for greater co-operation between the Churches for Sunday services, eucharistic fellowship and mixed marriages. Subsequently a Joint Ecumenical Commission was established for this purpose (1981–85); it pointed out that such practical matters that had been raised could not be dealt with without also clarifying more substantial unresolved doctrinal and historical questions. They thought that it was particularly necessary to see the extent to which the mutual condemnations between the churches at the time of the Reformation were historically conditioned.

As a result of their study, they noted that the condemnations of the Protestants were against the scholastic positions prior to the Council, and that the Council of Trent was targeting positions from a list of errors that had been drawn from the *404 theses* and the *Confutato*. In addition, some had been drawn up second or third hand. They suggested that, while no anathemas were given on the Protestant side after the Augsburg Diet, it was necessary to examine the anathemas of the Council of Trent, and to seek to identify the view against which these anathemas were directed: it was important to examine whether such descriptions or statements of doctrine were in any way misunderstood. This involved looking at these formulations afresh outside of the historical context and controversy and examining if both sides were saying the same things—but with different words—or words that had different meanings. Were the statements themselves on either side contradictory or in any way complementary? The authors oversaw joint studies to examine three complex areas of faith and justification, the sacraments, and the question of ministry. They left aside the articles of the Augsburg Confession which were not articles of faith but, in the mind of Melanchthon, were areas considered in need of debate, such as monasticism, the veneration of the saints and questions of Mariology. On the 24/5 October 1985, after several years of joint study, the chairman of the ecumenical study group was able to submit the whole undertaking to the Chairmen of the Joint Ecumenical Commission, Catholic Bishop Paul-Werner Scheele and Lutheran Bishop Eduard Lohse. The Report emphasized the gravity of the undertaking, as the Confessions of the 16th century were binding on all members of both churches, their leaders and members, and they directed how they viewed the other church. Because of their authoritative nature, they could "not be passed over in silence, or given a different interpretation, merely as we think best."[20]

## THE CONCLUSIONS OF THE REPORT: AN OPEN DOOR TO GREATER RECONCILIATION

The conclusions of the report were highly encouraging. Through hard work and fine forensic scholarly attention to detail they were able to conclude the following:

> The struggles of the Reformation period, in the dispute about the truth, led to different, indeed antithetical, forms of church doctrine. In the acrimony of the dispute, condemnations were uttered which, according to our now commonly acquired recognition, were even at that time the expression of an incomplete understanding of the facts on both sides. At all events, they no longer apply to today's partner. This means that the conditions have been created for clearing away severe hindrances which stand in the way of a closer community between the divided churches and for

20. Lehmann and Pannenberg, *The Condemnations of the Reformation* 179.

taking joint steps which can lead to a further strengthening and cementing of ecumenical community. The Joint Ecumenical Commission therefore asks the leading bodies of the churches involved to express in binding form that the sixteenth-century condemnations no longer apply to today's partner, inasmuch as its doctrine is not determined by the error which the condemnation wished to avert . . . As Christians belonging to the two churches encounter one another, they learn how to see the heritage of the other church in a new way. They direct their gaze toward the goal before them, which is to arrive at full community.

Maria Laach, 26 October, 1985 The Protestant and Catholic Chairmen of the
> Joint Ecumenical Commission:
> Eduard Lohse Paul-Werner Scheele[21]

In these wonderful concluding words, we see a path that can help heal so many wounds inflicted during the Reformation period, by both sides. The authors recognized the help and leading of the Holy Spirit in all their efforts, and that the results were indeed unprecedented. They suggest such statements would have been inconceivable fifty years previously. They felt the Holy Spirit had enabled them to clear pathways for greater Christian Unity. Without admission of heavy guilt and requisite repentance, they also agreed they unfortunately would need to stay 'eternally divided and opposed, one to the other.'[22]

One might conclude by using a symbol of architectural restoration. The Dresden Frauenkirche was completely devastated by the allied bombing of February 13th, 1945. By a similar vision of restoration and endless dedication, it has painstakingly been restored to its former glory. It is a symbol for us of a reconciled and united Church which we must also seek to build from the ruins of our history.

---

21. Lehmann and Pannenberg, The *Condemnations of the Reformation*, 186–87
22. Lehmann and Pannenberg, *The Condemnations of the Reformation*, 20

## Una Sancta

The Dresden Frauenkirche before and after its restoration 1945–2005

# 13

## The Academic Path to Unity after Vatican 2

JUST AS THE TIDE of unity went out after the time of the Augsburg Diet, it slowly started to come back in the 20th century and would start to become visible after Vatican II. The Council had an immediate effect on the ecumenical world which had drifted far apart with antithetical statements of doctrine. With fresh insight and academic research, people started to view the problems of the 16th century in a more balanced light. One of prime movers for greater recognition of the Augsburg Confession was University of Regensburg Professor of Dogma and the history of Dogma, Dr. Fr. Joseph Ratzinger. During the 1958–59 academic year he had introduced his students to the importance of the Augsburg Confession.[1] In turn, his work inspired one of his students, Catholic theologian Vincent Pfnür, to speak of a possible recognition of the CA at the International Catholic-Lutheran dialogue in Rome. The idea started to spread, and the request was then made to the German Bishop's Conference to "examine the possibility of a recognition of the Augsburg Confession by the Catholic Church". Approaches were also made by High Church Lutherans to the Secretariate for Christian

---

1. It is interesting to note that the last attempt to create agreement between the Reform and the Church also happened at Regensburg. It was as if Ratzinger was picking up the torch of reconciliation where it had last been dropped. See Chapter 8 p. 60 and the Ratisbon Colloquy of 1541

Unity in Rome for the Confession to be shown to be a Catholic confession, and suggestions made for a fresh examination of the Confession itself by competent theologians. Little by little, both Catholic and Lutheran theologians joined the discussion and shared their ideas across Germany, while the Lutheran World Federation recommended that Lutheran Churches "show an openness to and an interest in the Catholic recognition of the Augsburg Confession". An understanding of the Confession was beginning to be seen as a keyway through the historical impasse between Catholics and Lutherans. Central to this was a lecture given in 1976 in Graz Austria by Ratzinger himself, now as Archbishop of Munich and Freising. In it he declared that the Confession must be regarded as a central reference point. It was...

> not a document drafted for diplomatic reasons in such a way as would be considered as Catholic under Imperial Law,' but 'rather as a search with inner conviction for evangelical Catholicity fashioned in such a way to bring the early Reformation movement to help shape Catholic reform.' He continued to state that 'a Catholic recognition of the *Confessio Augustana* - or more correctly a recognition of the CA as Catholic—would help make corporate unification possible even in the face of differences. Such recognition by the Catholic Church would be much more than just a theological acceptance negotiated by historians and Church politicians, but rather a concrete spiritual decision which would be a new historical step on both sides'[2]

What was remarkable in all of this was how the 'chessboard' of moves to create unity had changed from the time in Augsburg in 1530. The Evangelicals had *initially* proposed the CA as a basis for discussion and debate: now it was the Catholic side proposing this move and suggesting that the CA was a Catholic Confession (which indeed it was always intended to be!). However, at this time only a few Lutheran groups were in favor of such a development: to many, such an idea was confusing, as the *Confutato* of Eck and others seemed to close forever such possible recognition. However, Lutherans had to see afresh that the CA "wished to be a witness of the whole church for the whole Church" and that the "Confession bound Lutherans to all other Christians of the world in one holy universal Christian

---

2. Archbishop Josef Ratzinger *Prognosen für die Zukunft des Ökumenismus* 39–41 https://unipub.uni-graz.at/oekf/content/titleinfo/1889472/full.pdfof

Church."³ The Lutheran World Federation took the lead: at their Assembly in Dar-es-Salaam in June 1977 they discussed to idea and passed a resolution. Under the title *Recognition of the Confession Augustana by the Roman Catholic Church,* they stated:

> The Assembly takes cognizance of the fact that distinguished Roman Catholic theologians consider it possible for their church to recognize the *Confessio Augustana* as a particular expression of the common Christian faith. They hope that this recognition would open the way toward a form of fellowship between the Roman Catholic Church and the Lutheran Church in which both churches, without abandoning their particularities and identities, would further the development towards full ecclesial communion as sister churches. The Assembly-conscious of the importance of this initiative- welcomes endeavors which aim at a Catholic recognition of the *Confessio Augustana*, expresses the willingness of the Lutheran World Federation to engage in dialogue with the Roman Catholic Church on this subject, and requests that the Executive Committee promote and carefully follow the progress of all studies of this matter, its possibilities, its problems, and its wider ecumenical implications."⁴

An important facet in all of this new movement towards unity was that the CA was "the least polemical and most conciliatory of all the Lutheran documents." Ratzinger said the "CA was a picture of Lutheranism 'in a state of repose, not distorted by excitement, distrust and dispute. It was for these reasons it was so readily accepted by all Lutheran Churches."⁵

## THE SCHLOSS SCHWANBERG MEETING 1976

One fruitful meeting point for Catholic and Lutheran theologians to discuss their differences regarding the Confession was organized by the High Church Society of the Augsburg Confession; it was held in Schloss Schwanberg, a Lutheran Ecumenical center in Rödelsee in Bavaria. They sought to tease out together questions that had to be answered for Catholic recognition of the Confession. The editors of the Ökumenische Information of the Catholic Press Service (KNA) and the Johann-Adam- Möehler Institute

---

3. Burgess *The Role of the Augsburg Confession* Introduction, xiii

4. Burgess *The Role of the Augsburg Confession* Introduction xiii Words of the Secretary and President of the LWF in Dar Es Salaam 1977

5. Burgess *The Role of the Augsburg Confession* Introduction .xv

in Paderborn asked the Catholic and Lutheran theologians present at the meeting to write a series of essays regarding possible Catholic recognition of the *Confessio Augustana*. The collection of essays was called *The Role of the Augsburg Confession* and was published in 1977 and edited by Joseph A. Burgess.[6] Contributions amongst others were from Heinz Schütte, Professor at Bonn University, Walter Kaspar, Professor at the University of Tubingen (and later Chairman of the Pontifical Council for Christian Unity), and Avery Dulles S.J., Professor at the Catholic University of America.

Vinzenz Pfnür (1937–2012), who spoke at the Conference, was Professor at the University of Münster and had been a student of Father (and subsequently Archbishop) Ratzinger at Regensburg University. Pfnür wrote the opening essay of the collection entitled "Recognition of the Augsburg Confession by the Catholic Church." He witnessed that ecumenical dialogue was gaining pace, with "ten important common declarations on what was"—until then—"seemingly insoluble controversial questions concerning Eucharist, Ministry created by various interconfessional groups of theologians."[7] One such dialogue which set the pace was commissioned by the United States Conference of Catholic Bishops (USCCB) Commission for Ecumenical and Interreligious affairs and the Lutheran World Federation (LWF). They produced documents on the historic creeds, the Eucharist as 'Sacrifice' and on the question of ministry. In March 1974 they issued a joint volume on the 'vexed' question of *Papal Primacy and the Universal Church* which showed great irenic sensitivity. Pfnür took up the challenge, initially given by Ratzinger. In the light of these interchurch agreements of the USCCB and the LWF, he questioned whether both sides were now willing to take further steps towards greater reconciliation and mutual recognition. He cited the joint volume where it stated:

> Even given these disagreements and points yet to be examined, it is now proper to ask, in the light of the agreement we have been able to reach, that our respective churches take specific actions toward reconciliation. Therefore we ask the Lutheran churches:
>
> - if they are prepared to affirm with us that papal primacy, renewed in the light of the gospel, need not be a barrier to reconciliation;

---

6. Burgess Joseph A. Ed. *The Role of the Augsburg Confession*. Fortress Philadelphia 1977/1980

7. Burgess *The Role of the Augsburg Confession*, 1

- if they are able to acknowledge not only the legitimacy of the papal ministry in the service of the Roman Catholic communion but even the possibility and the desirability of the papal ministry, renewed under the gospel and committed to Christian freedom, in a larger communion which would include the Lutheran churches;
- if they are willing to open discussion regarding the concrete implications of such a primacy to them.

Likewise, we ask the Roman Catholic Church:

- if in the light of our findings, it should not give high priority in its ecumenical concerns to the problem of reconciliation with the Lutheran churches;
- if it is willing to open discussion of possible structures for reconciliation which would protect the legitimate traditions of the Lutheran communities and respect their spiritual heritage;
- if it is prepared to envisage the possibility of a reconciliation which would recognize the self-government of Lutheran churches within a communion;
- if, in the expectation of a foreseeable reconciliation, it is ready to acknowledge the Lutheran churches represented in our dialogue as sister churches which are already entitled to some measure of ecclesial communion.[8]

As a definite step forward in the long road back to unity, the International Lutheran-Catholic working group in Rome in January 1974 had suggested that the Catholic church recognize the CA as a witness to the church's faith. This idea was then further taken up, as reported previously, by the Diocesan Ecumenical Commission of Munster at the meeting of 19th June 1974. They proposed:

> the German Conference of Bishops might examine the possibility of the Catholic Church recognizing the CA. Such a recognition would first, take the CA seriously in its historical and contemporary significance as an expression of the Protestant-Lutheran faith; at the same time it would dismantle a Catholic view of Lutheranism which is determined above all by polemically exaggerated Reformation expressions which stem from the period of radical change and disruption between 1520 and 1521 and which are preserved in collections of heretical Reformation statements, even

---

8. USCCB and LWF *Papal Primary and the Universal Church*, Augsburg Publishing 1974 par 31–33

though these, in the meantime, had already been corrected in the CA. Secondly, such a recognition would be an acknowledgment that the CA advocates no church-dividing teachings and that it can be affirmed on the Catholic side as a witness to the faith of the Church universal.[9]

What the Bishops recognized in this, is that common Catholic and Lutheran views of the time had been distorted by the polemically charged statements of the early Reformation period. In the Bishops' view, a recognition of the value of the CA would correct this distorted picture. The different sides in the Reformation needed to evaluate this whole period together to avoid distortion, exaggeration and outbursts which clouded reasonable discourse. Pfnür regrets the historical distorted baggage and how it influenced descriptions of the time, especially in Catholic textbooks. As an example, Pfnür uses thirteen page description of the Reformation and Counter Reformation taken a from the German Catholic textbook *Von Jesus bis Heute*. In this section, much is made of the young Luther diatribes, but there is no mention whatsoever of the CA. To place the early Luther in relation to the description of the Churches of the Reformation is to Pfnür "an ecumenically unacceptable short circuit."[10] Despite the progress in Luther studies by Lortz and others, Pfnür finds that "the theses already propounded by Johannes Cochläus remains almost self-evident: the criterion for studying the 'Reformation' is the early writings of Luther and Melanchthon. What is also inferred by this is that the CA "is not a full expression of the Protestant view."[11]

In this regard, it seems we have not moved much from the discourse at Augsburg, the 404 theses of Eck, and the Confutado. To Pfnür, "this is a perversion of the situation when seen by the unprejudiced spectator." Luther was indeed the spark which set so many groups ablaze with a variety of both Christian, orthodox *and* what would be considered heretical views— much of which were caught up in more political power struggles. After a period, the established Reformation could not engage with such distorted and heretical sidelines and issues: the essential elements of the Reformation needed to be clarified and expounded and the CA was the result which presented a "summary of our teaching."[12]

---

9. KNA-Ökumenische Information, No.6 Feb 1974 10–11.
10. Burgess *The role of the Augsburg Confession*, 5
11. Burgess, *The Role of the Augsburg Confession*, 5
12. Melanchthon, *Confession*, 32

As can be seen there is nothing that varies from the Scriptures or from the Church universal or the Church of Rome as known from its writers. Since this is so, those who insist that our teachers are to be regarded as heretics judge us too harshly.[13]

Pfnür concludes as follows: stating that the measure of what was truly Lutheran was established in the CA, raises it "above the multitude of Reformation pamphlets and polemical works written for particular occasions".[14] Cochlaeus claimed *the reverse* to be true—that the true nature of the Reformation was found in the early Luther writings, and that the CA was an insincere "totally insidious and devilishly deceptive maneuver." Pfnür states that this thesis can no longer be maintained.[15] Indeed, Melanchthon corrected the views that were held by Luther and others in the combustible atmosphere of the early reform in Wittenberg. At that time, in the zeal of conversion, all statements of traditional faith were being examined, debated and sometimes disregarded or rejected.

## THE JESUS REVOLUTION

One might compare this to the much less politically charged Jesus Revolution of the 1960's-70's in California. Much good fruit did indeed come from this revival of the hippies which had reached the front page of Time Magazine at that time. The movement, however, certainly seemed bizarre to conservative Church goers. An underground magazine of the time gave an invitation to young people which read:

> *God, King of Kings, Lord of Lords, Prince of Peace, Etc.*
> Notorious leader of an underground liberation movement
> Wanted for the following charges:
> Practicing medicine, winemaking and food distribution without a license.
> Interfering with businessmen in the temple.
> Associating with known criminals, radicals, subversives, prostitutes and street people.
> Claiming to have the authority to make people into God's children.
> Appearance: Typical hippie type-

---

13. Melanchthon, *Confession*, 32
14. Burgess, *The Role of the Augsburg Confession*, 6
15. Burgess, *The Role of the Augsburg Confession*, 6

long hair, beard, robe, sandals. Hangs around slum areas, few rich friends, often sneaks out into the desert.

Beware: This man is extremely dangerous. His insidiously inflammatory message is particularly dangerous to young people who haven't been taught to ignore him yet, He changes men and claims to set them free.

Warning: He is still at Large![16]

The movement had many branches, from the more orthodox Catholic charismatics quoted earlier, to Campus Crusade for Christ, and groups of communes and travelling hippie missionaries. Not all were orthodox: some groups were infused with the chiliast idea of an immediate return of Christ in the Second Coming and were preparing for possible collapse of the social system. Others advocated a Gnostic Docetism 'drop-out' culture, casting all of society- culture, social, governmental and education systems as being evil and in the complete grip of the devil. It seems that whenever there is genuine revival,—which one might recognize in both the Reformation and the Jesus Revolution,—there are also heretical ideas that surface. It took time for many who experienced the Jesus Revolution to jettison some of these views in favor of Christian orthodoxy, and thus it would be unfair to judge the Revolution by some of the earlier heretical ideas that flourished when the movement began. The writer of the article in Time Magazine draws an apt conclusion regarding the 'Revolution', quoting the famous British writer and former Catholic Chaplain to Oxford University, Monsignor Ronald Knox:

> In a world filled with real and fancied demons for the young, the form of their faith takes may be less important than the fact that they have it. Ronald Knox, who set out in *Enthusiasm* to expose the heresies of religious enthusiasts, concluded by praising their spirit. 'How nearly we thought we could do without St. Francis, without St. Ignatius,' he ended his work. 'Men will not live without vision; that moral we would do well to carry away with us from contemplating, in so many strange forms, the record of the visionaries.' Enthusiasm may not be the only virtue but, God knows, apathy is none at all.'[17]

---

16. *Time Magazine* June 21 1971 56 ffl.

17. *Time Magazine* June 21 1971 63 *Enthusiasm* was the title of his book on Church movements.

The CA demonstrates a similar development of doctrine from the early writings of Luther. For example, the early Reformation was prepared for churches to be directed or ruled by secular authorities. However, in the CA in Article 28, Melanchthon shows his lack of confidence in the competency of the secular authorities to regulate the Gospel, and felt that the destiny of the Church would be much better preserved with the Bishops.[18] Luther was supportive of Melanchthon's 'corrective'; writing from Coburg on 15 May 1530 he states: "I have read over Master Phillips Apologia: it pleases me very much and I don't know how to improve of change it, nor would it be suitable since I cannot tread so lightly or gently. Lord grant that it will bear much great fruit, as we hope and ask. Amen."[19]

It was Melanchthon who was able to create a solid orthodox doctrinal basis for the Reformation experience; truly, June 1530 is the real anniversary of the Reformation. If we are to choose the dates of 1517–1522 for marking the Reformation, we have to perforce take into account the "exaggerated position of Luther at this time, namely his philosophical determinism and his pessimism regarding sin."[20] Unfortunately, the same polemically exaggerated statements of Luther and the Reformers were "systematically collected" in a series of catalogues. These were then used as a starting point to the Council of Trent discussion of the Reformation. Even though the CA had systematically revised these in the Confession, the Reformation doctrines in the CA did not elicit any discussion at Trent. Sadly, another fact which distorted the Catholic understanding of the Reformation was the indiscriminate attacks on Catholic churches and clergy in the name of the new teaching. For some, it would be hard to dissociate such bigoted behavior from either the work of Luther or Melanchthon.

Pfnür summarized that Catholic recognition of the CA would stand in the forefront rather than "isolated, polemically exaggerated Reformation statements from what was a period of revolutionary change."[21] This would cause a whole unprecedented paradigm shift in the Catholic understanding of this troubled period. Once again, we turn to Archbishop Ratzinger (later Pope Benedict XVI) who in many ways had helped to create a much more hopeful and positive view of the whole Reformation period.

18. Melanchthon *The Augsburg Confession* 46–47
19. Bente *Project Wittenberg*, 23
20. Pfnür in Burgess *The Role of the Augsburg Confession*, 9
21. Pfnür in Burgess *The Role of the Augsburg Confession* 10

Generally the reality of the Church is seen as that which really divides, and in many respects it is. But one must not forget that it is not only the Roman Catholic Church and the various churches of the East which wish to be 'catholic' churches in the sense of the Church of the first centuries. It is also the Reformation churches, especially those of the CA, who sought and still seek genuine and primitive catholicity. This means that despite the differences of theological interpretation and the differences in historical starting points within the individual confessions, an astonishingly similar life exists, positively and negatively. Just as the humanity of man always manifests itself in a similar way under various signs, so, despite all divisions, the essential Christian content has always prevailed with astonishing uniformity.[22]

## THE 450TH ANNIVERSARY OF THE CONFESSION IN 1980: GROWING VOICES FOR RECOGNITION

Other contributors to *The Role of the Augsburg Confession* book looked with a measure of excitement of what was going to be the 450th anniversary of the CA in 1980.

Cardinal Walter Kasper (1933-) President Emeritus of the Pontifical Council for Promoting Christian contributes more to the argument for recognition of the CA by the Catholic Church. He sees recognition of the CA as more than a theological reception but an official act; it would *not* mean that the Catholic Church takes the CA as its own Roman Catholic expression; instead, it would be allowed as *one* legitimate expression of the common Catholic faith, so that the ecclesial community that appeals to it would be given room within the unity of the Catholic Church. "Nothing more" he says, "but nothing less than this was intended by its presentation to the Emperor Charles V at the Diet of Augsburg."[23] While Kasper sees that only the scriptures themselves can give the basis for unification, Catholic recognition of the CA can be an important step towards this unity.

Wolfhart Pannenberg (1928–2014) a Lutheran Professor who studied under Karl Barth says "If the Magisterium of the Catholic Church were to find itself in a position to confirm . . .through the ordinary teaching of its Bishops, or through a papal or conciliar pronouncement this (Catholicity

---

22. Ratzinger , Was eint und was trennt die Konfession. Communio 1 (1972)
23. Kasper in Burgess *The Role of the Augsburg Confession* 125

of the CA) . . . (it would be) of much more than historical interest. It would be an event of immense contemporary ecumenical significance . . .placing the ecumenical dialogue on an entirely new footing, not only with Lutheran Protestantism but with Protestants as a whole."[24]

American theologian Avery Dulles S.J (1918–2009) sees the recognition of the CA as helping to bring unity also to Anglicans and Presbyterians, as the CA was used in the formulation of the 39 Articles of the Anglican Church, and the Confession Variata of the Swiss Reformers. He dismisses that the Confutato has any relevance for today as the Roman theologians centered their objections on the last seven articles which Melanchthon regarded as abuses rather than as doctrines. To Dulles, "to a great extent these practices have been so changed that the objections cannot simply be repeated today."[25] He concludes in saying "thus the time may not be far away when it will be possible for Catholics and Lutherans, without loss of their distinctive identities and without reaching full agreement on all doctrines, to recognize each other as belonging to the same ecclesial fellowship. Such a mutual recognition would be of vastly greater significance than a Catholic recognition of the CA. But if such recognition and ecclesial fellowship ever comes about, there is no doubt that the CA, thanks to its simultaneously Catholic and Lutheran character, will have prepared the way."[26]

Heinz Schutte (1923–2007) from Paderborn, who played a significant role in the preparation of the *Joint Declaration on the Doctrine of Justification* in 1999, sees that it is totally understandable that the CA is discussed as a possible basis for agreement. Looking also to the anniversary of 1980, he notes the Chairman of the Commission on ecumenism of the Lutheran World Federation, Bishop Hermann Dietzfelbinger (1908–1984) said that Lutheran Churches need to prepare carefully for the discussion of the CA as a common confession,—especially in view of so many changes in the Catholic church since the time of the Reformation. Despite growing enthusiasm for a 'Catholic reception of the CA,' Schutte was completely aware of the difficulty that this would pose. He considered the many issues that would need to be analyzed and debated, including critical points made by the Protestant community itself today on the CA, how Luther's own theology in his time related to the CA and how to interpret the CA correctly in

---

24. Pannenberg in Burgess *The Role of the Augsburg Confession* 30
25. Dulles in Burgess *The Role of the Augsburg Confession*, 133
26. Dulles in Burgess *The Role of the Augsburg Confession*, 138

the light of different opinions[27]. Schutte however was of the opinion, that none of these points are obstacles to a recognition of the CA, and that all can be analyzed with time and patience.[28] He suggested a joint preparation of a commentary which would outline ideas which are either corrective or complimentary, together with a joint description of what would constitute unity and liberty. This whole process he envisioned would require much prayer for unity in truth and love. This would require repentance for, without a spirituality which is ecumenical and open to the Holy Spirit, the unity of the Church of Jesus Christ would not be possible.[29] Spiritual ecumenism he states must be viewed as "the soul of the whole ecumenical movement," as the Catholic Conference of German bishops in 1976 had emphasized, citing Vatican II.[30]

Joseph Ratzinger stated his assessment of the prospects of realizing corporate unity between the Lutheran churches and the Catholic Church:

> A Christianity of faith and faithfulness seeks unity; it lives its faith as a definite decision about its content and is precisely for this reason in search of unity. This is a faith which makes the highest demands on a person, renders him utterly powerless, and requires his unlimited patience and readiness for ever-renewed cleansing and deepening. But then, it so happens that Christianity rests entirely on the victory of the improbable, on the adventure of the Holy Spirit, who leads man beyond himself and precisely in this way leads him to his true self. Because we trust this power of the Holy Spirit, we therefore hope for the unity of the Church and put ourselves at the disposal of the ecumenism of faith.[31]

One other writer in the book *The Role of the Augsburg Confession* was Harry McSorley (1931–2017), Professor Religious Studies at St Michael's College, Toronto from 1970–1997. He became a Paulist priest and was one of the first North American clergy sent to study Protestant theology at the Johann Adam-Möhler Institute in Paderborn and at the University of Münich. In light of the changing ecumenical atmosphere following the

---

27. At a meeting the Author attended in Coburg Germany in April 2024 organized by Una Sancta Munich several difficulties were posed by attending Lutherans on the acceptance of the CA by Lutherans today without significant changes to the text.

28. Schütte in Burgess *The Role of the Augsburg Confession* 50–51

29. Schutte in Burgess *The Role of the Augsburg Confession* , 63

30. Ökumenisches Direktorium, Part III, following *Unitatis Redintegratio* 8 at Vatican 2

31. Ratzinger Prognosen für die Zukunft des Ökumenismus. 12

Council, he re-read the theological work of Dr Martin Luther which prepared him for many further years of service in the US Lutheran-Roman Catholic dialogue. Among his many points in his essay *Catholic recognition of the Confession Augustana: Precedents, Problems and Probabilities* he pointed to the growing consensus of scholars that Luther was "not only a sincerely Christian person, but also one who in his central and original Reformation protest was a Catholic reformer of the Church. Only through a complex set of tragic circumstances—involving what Vatican II calls 'fault on both sides'—did Luther's reform movement within the Catholic Church become a *Protestant* or *Lutheran* movement apart from full communion with the Church of which the Bishop of Rome is the chief earthly pastor"[32]. Because of this growing consensus and indeed multiplication of agreed documents, Mc Sorley looked forward "to a celebration event manifesting our growing oneness in Christ to share what God had been doing in our midst, to further an effective mutuality of witness, to seek ways in service to others to be more obedient Christians together."[33] The big hope he nurtured would be that on June 25 1980—the 450th anniversary of the Confession- the Roman Catholic Church could, in some ecumenical sense, "receive the CA as a legitimate type of Christian truth." However, McSorley felt that this could not happen by 1980, as all aspects of such a recognition would have to be thoroughly analyzed by the Roman Catholic Church. However, he saw the need for Catholics to take a much more positive attitude to the CA than they had had previously. He saw some of the following as helpful points towards that hopeful day of mutual recognition. Firstly—contrary to most conceptions of the Diet, an extraordinary degree of consensus was established between the Reformers and the Roman Church, not only on justification, but on practically all other doctrinal issues. Melanchthon and Luther had already indicated that they saw no major difficulties between the Confession and the Confutato. While John Eck is often viewed as the most vociferous Catholic apologist, he however states that of all the 21 articles of the first part of the CA, 'consensus was reached on all but two of the 19 articles' [that were discussed].[34] McSorley added "Surely the remarkable precedent of an 'almost' Catholic recognition of the CA 450 years ago should both encourage and challenge Catholics to complete the task in this

---

32. McSorley in Burgess *Role of the Augsburg Confession* ,139
33. McSorley in Burgess *Role of the Augsburg Confession*, 140
34. McSorley in Burgess *Role of the Augsburg Confession*, 141

time of ecumenical grace?"³⁵ The second point McSorley asked is: "What would such an agreement mean?" The very least, he said, would be that the Church recognizes that the CA contains a confession of faith of the Catholic Church, and that it also acknowledges new experiences and spiritual understanding that belong to the whole Catholic Church. Such recognition would not mean the CA is regarded as a full confession of the Catholic faith no more than either the Apostles Creed or the Nicene Creed are also full expressions of that faith.³⁶

The one difficulty he foresaw is the problem of reconciling all the Lutheran doctrinal statements of the Book of Concord with the CA. McSorley notes that Archbishop Ratzinger asked the same question. How does the CA in fact relate to the other Lutheran Confessional books and how firm is the unity of the Book of Concord, the Lutheran Collection of Documents from 1580? Mc Sorley asks, quoting Edmund Schlink, "Surely the Confession as a voice of the Church should be heard first before the individual Christian lifts his own voice to speak?" When Ratzinger pointed out the contradictions of the Smalcald Articles to the CA, McSorley said that Catholics are not being asked to recognize them,- indeed plenty of Lutherans do not either. While Ratzinger warned that recognition of the CA by 1980 would be premature, McSorley maintained that efforts towards recognition of the CA in a properly nuanced manner should...awaken true ideas about unity between Catholics and Lutherans. He quotes none other than Johann Eck—a man he says who "rejected every compromise at the expense of truth,"—who wrote to the Archbishop of Mainz after the Confutation. He said that "if we could have discussions with them (Reformers), I believe concord would immediately take place on the other 22 articles."³⁷

In 1977 Mc Sorley concluded that, barring some Divine intervention, that neither would the Catholic and Lutheran Churches be re-united, nor would the CA be recognized as being Catholic at that time. However, he was hopeful that after the long years of division, that the commitment to both goals would be strengthened. Surely, he states "Catholics and Lutherans should hope for nothing less when they gather for prayer and dialogue in Augsburg and elsewhere."³⁸

---

35. McSorley in Burgess *Role of the Augsburg Confession*, 141

36. McSorley in Burgess *Role of the Augsburg Confession*, 143

37. McSorley in Burgess *The Role of the Augsburg Confession*, 147 quoting Pfnür, Enig 256 ' *Credo statim fieret concordia in aliis XXII articulus.*'

38. Mc Sorley in Burgess *The Role of the Augsburg Confession* 147

# The Academic Path to Unity after Vatican 2

## 'CONFESSING ONE FAITH' THE JOINT GERMAN STUDY AND AMERICAN PUBLICATION

Probably one of the most exciting analyses of the CA as a valid Catholic Confession was created in Germany and then presented in the United States. While there had been many discussions, papers and meetings on the Confession, it was felt that it was necessary to have more than commentaries by individual Catholic and Lutheran authors. A growing consensus felt that it was necessary to facilitate a *common* Catholic Lutheran interpretation of the Confession. Four theologians ( two Catholic and two Lutheran) agreed together to take on this project. Together they spread the idea to interested parties across Germany and the United States; by 1978 they had arranged for 22 theologians from both Church communities to give their joint perspectives on the 28 Articles of the Confession. In so doing, they managed to achieve a high level of consensus in declaring 'one faith'; this was effectively the first time that something like this had happened since the Confession itself was written by Melanchthon in 1530. Two of the leaders of the group who wrote the introduction to the German version—Harding Meyer and Heinz Schütte- made it clear from the outset, however, that their common enterprise was *not* an official undertaking of the churches. Rather, the work and conclusions were the responsibility of the authors themselves.[39] Their hope was that this academic work would be "of service to the churches." Although they noted there were, in fact, many publications on the 'Catholicity' of the CA by numerous mainly German authors, until this time there had been no common Catholic-Lutheran effort to interpret the Confession.

The authors very soon found support, and their initial four theologians grew to eight, each willing to work on such a commentary and be part of a joint editorial board. Many of the writers assembled would have been well known names to those working on Catholic-Lutheran relationships, both in Europe and the States. They included Father (and later Cardinal) Walter Kasper who had been dean of Dogmatic Theology in both Münster and Tübingen Universities and later President of the Pontifical Council for the Promotion of Christian Unity, Father (and also later Cardinal) Lehmann, Professor of Dogmatic and Ecumenical Theology at the University of Freiburg, American Cardinal Avery Dulles, French theologian René Laurentin, and well known Lutheran theologians George Lindbeck of Yale who was a 'delegate observer' at the Second Vatican Council, and Bernhard

---

39. Forell and McCue, *Confessing One Faith*, 15

Lohse, Professor of Church History and Historical Theology at the University of Hamburg. Together they wished to determine, through joint scholarly investigation to what extent each of the 28 articles of the Augsburg Confession was capable of a joint Catholic-Lutheran understanding and interpretation.[40] . How did the authors evaluate the results of their initiative?

Firstly, they recognized the unique status of the CA as a binding document for all Lutheran churches: all other Lutheran foundational documents (such as were found in the *Book of Concord*) were regarded as expositions of facets of its articles. Thus, any agreement on the CA was highly significant for all other Lutheran teaching. Whilst of great interest historically the CA is more than this: it stands as a witness to an agreement on the core of the Christian faith itself. The authors then proceeded to discuss the Catholicity of the AC. Here, in their words, are some of the key results of their research:

1. It is a conclusion of our common work that the CA not only had the intention of bearing witness to the common catholic faith but that to a large degree its assertions must actually be understood as an expression of that catholicity. Even where questions still remain open, convergences can be seen. That is; in reaching back to the CA we have arrived at a common understanding of the center of the Christian faith.

2. This consensus was especially evident where the beliefs in the Triune God and the saving work of Jesus Christ, which unite all Christendom, were concerned. Thus, we have again become aware that the church division of the 16th century had not gone to the roots.

3. ...The assertions of the CA concerning the church bind rather than separate us. They provide the basis for a common understanding of the holiness, catholicity, apostolicity and, with that, unity of the church. The constitutive marks of the church are founded on the right proclamation of the gospel and in an administration of the sacraments that is in keeping with Christ's institution, as well as in the office of ministry, which has been given to the church for the sake of those functions.

Finally they concluded:

4. The unity of the church is not something that human beings need to produce. However, the separated ecclesial communities can recognize each other again in the antecedently given unity of the one church which "is to continue forever" (perpetuo mansura). That obliges them

---

40. Forell and McCue Confessing one Faith, 14

to take steps toward a reconciliation and to ask whether the continuing separation can be justified before God.[41]

This work is indeed of great significance and gives great hope for the results of any continuing work we may see in the time leading to the 500th anniversary. How might we conclude the work of these authors and their American counterparts McCue and Forell?

The first thing that is apparent and gives one hope in viewing the submissions of *Confessing One Faith,* is that the synthesis of the Confession with the commentary is greater than the Confession alone—the sum is, in fact, greater than the parts. By combining the CA with the thoughtful irenic analysis of highly qualified Catholic and Lutheran theologians, the Ecclesiology and Christology of both communities of faith is thereby strengthened: it would seem the parts 'cross pollinate' in unexpected ways, drawing out the strength of both traditions. In a word—a hopeful word—it would seem that the CA was indeed a helpful contribution to the 16th century church, Had it been processed in a similar, but peaceful way, with the best of theologians, it could perhaps have had a great unified and reforming effect upon the whole Church of the time. Undoubtedly it would also have created a stronger united, more ecumenical Council of Trent and have avoided the schism and all its unfortunate results in European history. These thoughts are, of course, completely speculative, and there were many political overtones at the time of the Diet which are not evident today. Viewed outside of this, the challenge of the CA helps to clarify some church and faith issues. C.S. Lewis distilled basic Christianity in his 'Mere Christianity' and Nicky Gumbel also managed to do the same in his popular Alpha Course.[42] Both of these helps to shine a light on the core beliefs of Christianity away from routine, tradition and habit. The CA asks what should the church be? What is essential for it to function? What are its most basic beliefs? What is it to trust Christ for salvation? Why priests? Why Bishops? The CA may be seen to be functioning as a mirror to the Church to check that everything is in good order—for both the hierarchy and the ordinary lay person. That 22

---

41. Forell and McCue, *Confessing one Faith,*.334–38

42. C.S. Lewis popular classic ' Mere Christianity' was composed with approval of all British mainline denominations, Anglican, Catholic, Methodist and Presbyterian. The Alpha course very popular around the world today takes a similar approach using the core essentials of the Christian faith and has been successfully used by most main denominational and non-denominational churches. https://en.wikipedia.org/wiki/Alpha_course

highly qualified Catholic and Lutheran theologians could agree together, in such harmonious fashion, should give us great hope for the future and indeed for the plans for 2030.

Catholic-Lutheran unity didn't happen in 1980, nor was the CA recognized as being 'Catholic' at that time as McSorley foresaw. In spite of the 'cloud of witnesses' seeking for this rent in the garment of Christ to be recognized and healed for the 450th anniversary of the Confession, it did not eventuate. However, after the Joint Declaration of Justification of 1999, could we be hopeful that it might happen in 2030—the 500th anniversary of the Augsburg Confession?

# 14

# Breakthrough! 1999–2030?

AFTER MANY YEARS OF conversations in the spirit of the Una Sancta meetings hosted by Metzger during the war and continued by Archbishop Jaeger and Lutheran Bishop Wilhelm Stählin in Paderborn, before the work of Cardinal Bea and the Pontifical Council for Christian Unity, a wonderful visible breakthrough between Lutherans and Catholics occurred in the years 1998–99. Lutheran groups and Catholics finally had reached a point of consensus over the very doctrine that had divided them at the time of the Augsburg Confession. On June 16, 1998, the Council of the Lutheran World Federation and its standing committee on ecumenical affairs, stated that the Joint Statement that had been prepared by both sides of the Reformation schism:-

> is a result of a process involving both the action of the affirming churches and the action of the LWF Council. [It recommended that] the agreements regarding the doctrine of justification as presented in the 'Joint Declaration' be affirmed, and that, on the basis of these agreements the doctrinal condemnations in the Lutheran confessional writings regarding justification be declared not to apply to the teaching of the Roman Catholic church as presented in the 'Joint Declaration'.[1]

---

1. Wood a Wengert, *Shared Spiritual Journey*, 58

One month later, on July 16th, 1998, Cardinal Edward Cassidy, the President of the Pontifical Council for Christian Unity, declared:

> It is for me a pleasure and source of much satisfaction to present today a document declaring that a consensus on fundamental truths regarding the doctrine of justification has been reached in the dialogue between the Catholic Church and the Lutheran World Federation. The present joint declaration has this intention: namely, to show that, on the basis of their dialogue, the subscribing Lutheran churches and the Roman Catholic Church are now able to articulate a common understanding of our justification by God's grace through faith in Christ.[2]

After some last-minute clarifications—the Agreement between the Churches was ready to be signed. History was made, and the two sides who had not been able to reach agreement on the wording of the Augsburg confession on June 25, 1530, met again in the same City of Augsburg on October 31st 1999. Together they signed the *Joint Declaration on the Doctrine of Justification* (JDDJ). This was the first time since the Reformation that representatives of the Catholic Church and the Lutheran church had agreed on a Doctrinal statement! It was a foundational stone of mutual Christian recognition by both sides of the Western schism. This was not the end of the story, but the beginning of a new chapter, for, as a consequence, there is not yet any visible unity between the churches of the Reformation. By dedicated hard work on both sides—something that was largely initiated by the work of Blessed Max Josef Metzger during World War II- a breakthrough was witnessed. Like many such breakthroughs in history they are not necessarily noticed at the time they occurred; not many people know of the JDDJ and even less have understood its import. In some ways it was like an echo of the 95 theses of Luther, when at the time there was a simple invitation of a Catholic University professor at the university to debate church reform but that subsequently exploded into a vital force that concluded thirteen years later in a church schism. The JDDJ has been a relatively quiet affair and not widely known across the Christian world, however it portends great hope for a growing consensus between Christians. Just, too, as Luther's Theses and the Augsburg confession helped to pave a path to the Anglican 39 Articles, the JDDJ 'in reverse' was welcomed by the Anglican Communion and affirmed the substance of the Joint Declaration on the Doctrine of Justification (JDDJ) in 2016. As the Augsburg Confession Variata helped in the

---

2. Wood and Wengert *Shared Spiritual Journey* .59

development of the Calvinist Church of Switzerland, the World Council of Reformed Churches (representing 80 million members of Congregational, Presbyterian, Reformed, United and Waldensian Churches), signaled their approval of the JDDJ on July 5th 2017.[3] The World Methodist Council signaled their approval of the Declaration on 23 July 2006 at their meeting in Seoul South Korea, making the Agreement a five-way confession of faith of major Christian confessions. The rent which was created in the seamless robe of Christ in 1530 had begun a quiet restoration and healing.

Of primary importance in this situation has been an overall change in the attitudes of Church leaders and ordinary Christians to one another: repentance and a need for forgiveness for past wrongs was necessary. From a Catholic point of view, all these events were unprecedented. In the entire history of the Church, there had not been any requests for forgiveness for the wrongs of the past by the Church itself. Whilst individual clerics and laymen had been censured by Papal decrees, sanctioned and corrected, very rarely had ecclesiastical authorities or Bishops, Councils, or the Pope himself acknowledged any faults or abuse of power for which they themselves were responsible. Church Jubilees, which had been introduced by Pope Boniface VIII in 1300, were occasions for sacramental pardon for sin and were regular occasions for a joyful celebration of the salvation given in Christ. However, in none of the Jubilees, from the 14th century to the 20th century (prior to Vatican II) was there any acknowledgement for any of the church's sins or a request to God for pardon for past misconduct. The Vatican issued a Document called *Memory and Reconciliation, The Church and the faults of the past* in December 1999, just before the new Millennium; it was proposed and signed by Cardinal Ratzinger, the Prefect of the Congregation for the Doctrine of the Faith. In it, the Church authorities gave the example of the reforming Pope Adrian who, at the Diet of Nuremburg on November 25th 1522, acknowledged publicly: "the abominations, the abuses... and the lies" of which the "Roman court" of his time was guilty, "deep-rooted and extensive... sickness," extending "from the top to the members."[4]

While Pope Adrian VI excoriated the faults of his times, and especially those of his immediate predecessor Leo X and the Vatican curia (who had overseen the excommunication of Luther) he did not ask for pardon

---

3. The Augsburg Confession Variata was a later version of the AC which includes differences in understanding with Communion more in keeping with the beliefs of Calvinists.

4. https://www.vatican.va/roman_curia/congregations/cfaith/cti_documents/rc_con_cfaith_doc_20000307_memory-reconc-itc_en.html

on behalf of the Church itself. Time had to wait for Pope Paul VI in the 20th century who expressed such regret for past behavior, both to God and to the assembled members of the Vatican Council and representatives of other 'separated' churches. He solemnly asked, "pardon of God . . . and of the separated brethren" of the East who may have felt offended "by us" (the Catholic Church) and declared himself ready for his part to pardon offences received. By this statement, he was opening a reciprocal exchange to heal the wounds of division of the Church.[5]

Pope Saint John Paul II continued this path, established by his predecessors and the Vatican Council in his Apostolic Letter *Tertio Millennio Adveniente*. In this, he extended a request for forgiveness 'to a multitude of historical events in which the Church or individual groups of Christians were implicated in different respects'. The Washington Post recorded:

> VATICAN CITY, March 12—In an unprecedented plea, Pope John Paul II today asked divine forgiveness for the sins committed by the Roman Catholic Church over the last 2,000 years against Jews, other Christian faiths, women, the poor and various ethnic and racial groups.
> 
> Dressed in a purple robe, the color of the Lenten period of penitence that began Wednesday, John Paul asked for the comprehensive pardon in an extraordinary ceremony at St. Peter's Basilica.
> 
> "We ask for forgiveness for the divisions that came between Christians, for the use of violence that some used in the service of truth, and for the attitudes of diffidence and hostility assumed before the followers of other religions," he said in his homily. He also called for forgiveness of those who had harmed or persecuted Christians.[6]

The tide of forgiveness and reconciliation was now firmly lapping on the shores of all Christian confessions in a wave of genuine love. The journalist noted that the pardon was general, with no more specific reference to past sins and sinners. "The inquisition, violence during the crusades, schisms with Protestants and the Orthodox, forced evangelization and the extermination of the Jews was alluded to but not mentioned in his Mass." The full meeting and reconciliation of Catholics and Lutherans has yet to

---

5. Recounted in Christianity Today https://www.christianitytoday.com/2008/08/forgive-and-remember/ August 2008. Accessed 10/28/2024

6. https://www.washingtonpost.com/archive/politics/2000/03/13/pope-asks-pardon-for-sins-of-church/9efdf34b-7912-489f-a6d0-b01eb57c64d6/ Accessed 10/28/2024

happen; how it will happen is not clear, but with determination and courage on all sides, one can pray that it will, indeed, occur.

So where does this leave us with the Church-dividing Confession of Augsburg? Surely this is the next step on the path of reconciliation between the churches. While such recognition would not mean Catholics and Lutherans would be one united church, it would mean that they both recognize each other in a deep way,—as one family in the process of healing. Joseph's reconciliation with his brothers was not instant; it needed to be processed and worked through. This seems to be the thinking of Pope Francis and leaders of the Lutheran World Federation. At a meeting in Krakow, Poland, on September 13–19, 2023, of the Assembly of the *Lutheran World Federation*—representing 150 Lutheran churches in 99 countries,- Cardinal Koch, the Prefect of the *Dicastery of Pontifical Council for Christian Unity* and the Federation's General Secretary, Rev. Anne Burghardt called for a joint Catholic-Lutheran reflection on the Augsburg Confession. Their statement, *A Common Word,* released by the USCCB stated that:

> Such "a common reflection could lead to another 'milestone' on the way from conflict to communion,". They stated the Augsburg Confession was drafted in 1530 in an attempt "to bear witness to the faith of the one, holy, catholic and apostolic church. At the time of its writing, ecclesial unity was probably endangered, but ecclesial separation was not yet finally accomplished." Because the statement of the Confession was meant to be a witness to Christian unity before the final schism of the Western Church, they said it was "not only of historical interest; rather, it holds an ecumenical potential of lasting relevance.". . . They agreed that such dialogue can allow both Catholics and Lutherans "to discern areas of consensus where our predecessors only saw insurmountable oppositions. We are able to recognize that the journey toward full communion is far greater than the contingencies of a particular epoch.[7]

The delegates also quoted the words of Pope Francis when he met the leaders of the LWF in 2021 that such a joint study of the Augsburg Confession in advance of the 500th anniversary of the Confession in 2030 could help Catholics and Lutherans "to confess together what joins us in faith. It will be important to examine with spiritual and theological humility the circumstances that led to the divisions, trusting that, although it is

---

7. USCCB Common Word. https://www.usccb.org/news/2023/vatican-lutheran-officials-call-joint-study-augsburg-confession

impossible to undo the sad events of the past, it is possible to reinterpret them as part of a reconciled history".⁸

Anticipating such a reality Lutheran Professor Timothy Wengert and Catholic Professor Sister Susan Wood wrote in their book ' A Shared Spiritual Journey"

> Perhaps now is the time for dialogue to concentrate its efforts on envisioning the shape of a reconciled church. The North American Orthodox-Catholic Theological Consultation engaged in such an exercise as one attempt to overcome an impasse over the issue of papal primacy. The theological work between Lutherans and Catholics has matured to the point that such practical envisioning in light of the church's location in time and place may be the logical next step in dialogue. Just as Lutherans sought ecclesial solutions to their ecclesial situation at the time of the Reformation, so now new ecclesial solutions must be identified by both Lutherans and Catholics to reflect a reconciled relationship in the twenty-first century.⁹

---

8. USCCB Common Word https://www.usccb.org/news/2023/vatican-lutheran-officials-call-joint-study-augsburg-confession

9. Wood S and Wengert T.*Spiritual Journey*. 206

# BREAKTHROUGH! 1999-2030?

**Cardinal Koch of the Dicastery for the Promotion of Christian Unity and Rev Anne Burghardt of the Lutheran World Federation reading the Common Statement at their meeting in Poland in September 2023.**

This summary of the history of the Augsburg Confession was written to encourage that recognition of the Confession as a Catholic and non-dividing Confession of faith. It would seem to be the next logical step to undo the damage which was created at the Diet of Augsburg. The break was so small to commence with: as we have seen nearly everything was agreed upon by the two sides. Such an agreement, in 2030, could represent an incremental step in what Wood and Wengert describes as an "ecclesial recognition of imperfect communion:"[10]

---

10. Wood S and Wengert T. *Spiritual Journey* 195

# Afterword
## A Reflection by Blessed Max Josef Metzger, Martyr for Christian Unity, Dresden Hofkirche November 1941.

THIS BOOK TAKES ITS subtitle from a talk given by Blessed Max Josef Metzger in the Dresden Catholic Hofkirche, on Sunday 16 November 1941. Metzger travelled extensively around Germany during the war, promoting his idea of *Una Sancta* and genuine ecumenical endeavor. Prior to the sermon he had been reading the latest novel by German poetess and author, Gertrud von le Fort, called *Die Magdeburgische Hochzeit* (The Magdeburg Wedding). Reading the novel caused Metzger great distress. The novel tells the tragic story of the sacking of the German city of Magdeburg on May 20th, 1631, by the Imperial Army and forces of the Catholic League, under the command of Johann Tilly and Gottfried of Pappenheim. The battle resulted in the death of over 20,000 citizens, including defenders and non-combatants. It was considered to be the worst atrocity of the Thirty Years War of 1618–1648, which was fought to eradicate Protestantism and enforce Catholicism throughout the Holy Roman Empire.

# Afterword

The Magdeburger Hochzeit or Magdeburg Wedding Painting by Matthäus Merian (1593–1650) Imperial Catholic troops conquer the Protestant city during the 30 years' war.

Prior to the war, Magdeburg was one of the biggest cities in Europe, with a population of 25,000. After the fire (which ended the siege), there were only an estimated 1,000 survivors, and a subsequent census of citizens accounted for only 450 people. The city lay in ruins until the 18th century. It was (sadly) described as a 'Catholic Victory', as the citizens of Magdeburg had become Lutheran in 1524, joining the Schmalkaldic League which had fought the policies of Emperor Charles V, the overseer of the Augsburg Diet in 1530. When the looting of the city ended on May 24th, Catholic Mass was once more celebrated in the Cathedral on the following day. The victorious Graf Pappenheim wrote in a letter, "I believe that over 20,000 were lost. It is certain that no more terrible work and divine punishment has been seen since the destruction of Jerusalem. All our soldiers became rich. God [is] with us." Pope Urban VIII wrote in a letter of congratulation to Tilly saying "You have washed your victorious hands in the blood of sinners."[1]

As Metzger read Gertrud's account of the sad retelling of the sack of Magdeburg whilst preparing for his address, he had cause to weep.

He asked: "Must the Christian faith be divided?" He then added that "the tragedy of the schism in Christianity does not end this guilt, even for present day Christians". He then described and reacted to the book as he gave in his Dresden speech:

---

1. Wikipedia *Magdeburg Wedding* The original Latin quote of the Pope read: "Potuisti lavare victrices manus in sanguine peccatorum." This quote paraphrased Psalm 58,10, (Psalm 57 in the Latin Vulgate). Taken from Meumann and Neifanger (1997).

## Afterword

Gertrud von Le Fort, one of the most gifted poets of our time, has written a profound novel: "The Magdeburg Wedding". The tragedy of the German religious schism has rarely been expressed as shockingly as in this work. For the "true faith" the two camps in Germany face each other for thirty bloody years, until Germany resembles more a desert than a blooming garden. Tilly, the "Catholic Excellency", is the Emperor's Generalissimo. He fights under the blue flag of the Blessed Virgin, and he wins at Magdeburg, the gate to Germany. The protesting city goes up in flames—contrary to Tilly's will—right down to the [Lutheran] cathedral. A victory is at the same time the greatest defeat. For the cruel bloody court drives the protesting estates finally into the camp of the Swedish enemy of the Empire.[2] The Emperor's "empire" falls apart, and in the end the "faith" is not served either... The conclusion of this work is downright magnificent. The "victory" is to be celebrated with the *Te Deum* in the cathedral. But the priest represents the true religion to Tilly: "How can one sing *Te Deum* over 20,000 corpses?" The "Catholic Excellency" himself is more interested in the De Profundis, but the treasury of the cruel logic of war no longer allows freedom. Anyone who wants to protect religion with the weapons of hell himself falls victim to the power of evil. It is not pride but love that conquers everything. This is the constantly misunderstood secret of the Virgin's banner: "Mary does not win with the sword in her hand, Mary wins with the sword in her heart, she wins through the suffering love of her beloved Son..." "Christ does not win in the fight against the cross, but on the cross... Christ can only win the cross of the schism on the cross of the schism... Christ only wins in the mystery of His love"

While the high mass is being celebrated in the cathedral, the Protestant preacher Bake, struggling to save his life, leaves the city. Then he heard the *"Credo in unum Deum..."* from the cathedral, which is also his creed. It forced him to his knees. For the first time in his life he was shocked to realize that, despite the division of the confessions, there was a unanimous confession of the whole of Christendom..." And hope blossomed in him for a new Germany, which had finally found peace again through the brotherly reflection of all its members on the common confession of the fathers, on a newly emerging love that will overcome all separation... The novel ends movingly, with the preacher who has been driven out

---

2. The city hoped that they would be aided by the Swedish Lutheran King, Gustavus Adolphus who had landed on the north German Coast on 6 July 1631. Augustus finally only took control of Magdeburg in December 1642, returning the city to the Lutheran faith.

## Afterword

of his cathedral praying together with the credo of his enemies that can be heard from afar: "*Confiteor unum baptisma in remissionem peccatorum.*"[3]

The original 'Mourning Magdeburg' was created for the City of Worms before a cast was created for Magdeburg where it was displayed in St John's Church in 1924 until the church was badly bombed during the air raids of World War 2. It once again sits in the entrance of the church. It depicts a mourning Virgin with a falling crown of Magdeburg on her head and a blunt, broken sword. It represents symbolically the destruction of Magdeburg for its commitment to the Protestant cause.

3. Text taken from a talk given on November 16 1941 in the Dresden Hofkirche by Blessed Max Josef Metzger called *Muß die Glaubenspaltung* Sein? Mission brief Nr 21 Christköeniggesselschaft vom WeißenKreutz. Supplied by Msgr Lubomir Žák, Director of Max Josef Metzger Center, Olomouc Czech Republic 2024. The Latin text means 'I believe in one Baptism for the remission of sins.'

# Afterword

Metzger concludes his description of Gertrud von Le Fort's novel by sharing his feeling alluding indirectly to the conflict that surrounded his audience at that time:

> I am not ashamed of the tears that overwhelmed me as I closed the book. Must it be that the cruel tragedy of those days continues through all the centuries? Must it be that in the name of the "true faith" the disciples of the same Lord, the Master of Love, face each other in incomprehension, even hostility, until the end of time? Must there be a division of Germany, the division of Christianity in general? Is there no way to close this gap and to realize the Lord's final will: "that all may be one!"? It does not have to be that way. But it will be that way until there is a conversion on all sides to the faith that is the deepest: redemption from all guilt and all evil is once and for all based on the sacrificial offering of Christ. And redemption from the evil of the schism in faith will only come when Christians remember this and find the courage to start anew with "humility" in the love of Christ.
>
> Not pride, not self-righteousness, love can do everything! If there had been no pride, if love had been alive in all those involved, the "Reformation" would have taken a different course.
>
> Why did they not want to admit that a reformation "in head and limbs" was necessary? Wasn't this even admitted in shocking words by Pope Adrian VI, the last German Pope, in his instruction to the legate Chieregati (1522)?[4] And why also [was it admitted] by calling the "Reform" Council of Trent? Wouldn't a superior Christian attitude on the part of all church authorities have led to the positive powers of the "Reformer" being made available to the entire Church in an essential renewal of Christianity? Isn't the lack of this partly to blame for the Reformation becoming a revolution that caused the Church's most valuable asset to perish, often against the will of the "Reformer"?[5]
>
> I once studied the personal testimonies of church figures in the period from 1517 to 1525. They were not the worst people who

---

4. Metzger here is speaking of Bishop Chieregati (1479–1539), the Papal Nuncio who worked for several Popes. Among the Popes was Pope Leo X, who had excommunicated Luther. Pope Adrian VI was the successor to Pope Leo and sent Chieregati to address the Diet of Nuremberg. In the address Pope Adrian berated the sins of the ecclesiastics who were the main cause of the troubles in the church. He did not spare either the Pope or the Curia from his critique, as all 'head and shoulders', he said had been guilty of abuse. The Diet avoided answering his message and instead continued to voice more grievances against the Catholic Church in Germany.

5. Metzger here is referring to Martin Luther as the 'Reformer'.

## Afterword

initially enthusiastically welcomed Martin Luther as a God-sent reformer of the church. But after just a few years, the same people were often complaining: It is not better, it has become worse than before. Who is to blame? Did the reformer lack humility, prudence, patience, love? Did he ultimately allow himself to be driven by ambition and self-righteousness? It is not up to us to judge. The sober historian finds that the "guilt" for the unfortunate schism in the faith does not lie on one side alone, that humaneness on both sides has often pushed the cross of Christ into the background and caused the love of the Lord to be forgotten...

Is it not time for all honest Christians to bear witness to the truth simply and humbly?

Would it not be truly Christian, "evangelical" and "catholic" at the same time, to start again where one abandoned the common path of Christ out of humanity? To remember again what is fundamentally common in the one faith and the one baptism through which one was once "one"? To become aware that all those baptized in the name of Christ have been incorporated into His "one body" as its members and, according to the Catholic view, belong to it if they faithfully follow the Lord according to their conscience? Even if conscience sometimes goes astray! Is it not more in keeping with the spirit of the Lord to rejoice in this existing, albeit imperfect, unity, instead of always seeing and emphasizing the divisions? Should not everyone always go to the Lord's school anew to examine whether the divisions are actually based on the "gospel" or perhaps often only on human thought that does not have the Lord's promises for itself? If the "Catholics" admit that some of the "theses" that were posted in Wittenberg in 1517 actually addressed abuses in the Church and legitimately demanded remedy, the others should ignore the fact that most of the concerns of the Reformation were directed at us Catholics: all of the legitimate concerns that have since been widely accepted and fulfilled in the Mother church and that many things that were sacred to Martin Luther were lost among his successors, but are better guarded in the Roman Church than "over there"? The salvation from the distress that, thank God, is burning in the souls of more and more people, is only given in one: Christ. In His truth and His love.

Away with all self-righteousness that does not seek Christ, but the victory of one's own opinion! Away with all prejudices that have been persistently dragged on here and there through the centuries, no matter how often they have already been scientifically eliminated! Away with the frivolity of mutual suspicion of honesty

## Afterword

and sincerity—it does not correspond to the Christian attitude! Trust in the good intentions and genuine willingness of the other is a duty of truthfulness and justice, as long as the opposite is not clearly proven! Humility is needed, which recognizes and admits the limitations of all human thought and research. Willingness to understand and appreciate the opposing side's point of view, not first of all to discover and appreciate the misunderstandings and errors, but above all to discover and appreciate the core of truth in the foreign view.

Of course, that alone does not lead to the goal. It would be a delusion to believe that only misunderstandings stand in the way of unification, that all that is needed is "good will" to put aside the theological subtleties and agree on the "essentials". There are essential differences that cannot simply be ignored by honest seekers of truth, nor can they easily be overcome by them. But there is no doubt that with mutual goodwill, much of what divides us today could be put aside. There is no doubt that many bridges could be built on which we can meet in understanding, and indeed, over which a mutual exchange could take place, enriching both sides.

Can an agreement be found in this way that will end the religious schism and unite all of Christ's followers in German lands again? Perhaps that is a false hope. Yes, human efforts will probably never succeed in lifting the curse

Only from the grace of God can we expect and ask for what is "impossible to man". But we can count on the grace of the Lord the more we ourselves remove all obstacles that stand in the way of this work. May we selflessly, humbly and lovingly go about the work that has somehow been given to us as a task by God:

That all may become one!

Blessed Maximillian Josef Metzger (1887-1944).[6]

---

[6]. Max Josef Metzger became Blessed Maximillian Metzger in a ceremony in Freiburg Cathedral on November 17th 2024. The Mass of Beatification was celebrated by Cardinal Koch, President of the Dicastery for the Promotion of Christian Unity. Text taken from *Muß die Glaubensspaltung Sein*.

Cardinal Arborelius of Sweden, Cardinal Koch of the Dicastery for the Promoting Christian Unity, Dr Martin Junge of the Lutheran World Federation, Palestinian Lutheran Bishop Munib A Younan and Pope Francis with Lutheran Archbishop Antje Jackelén in Lund Sweden at joint ecumenical commemoration of the 500th anniversary of the Reformation in 2017.

# About the Author

Dr Cormac O'Duffy the Dresden Hofkirche where Max
Josef Metzger spoke on November 16th 1941

**Cormac O'Duffy** is an American-born Irishman who grew up in Ireland
and the UK. He completed his university education in Ireland where he

## About the Author

received a Bachelor of Music from University College Dublin and an MA (Hons) and PhD from the University of Limerick. He works as a music director in a parish in South Carolina and as a composer. Most recently his oratorio *Metzger* was premiered on April 21 2024 in Brandenburg-Görden Prison in Brandenburg, where the now Blessed Max Josef Metzger (1887–1944) was executed on 17 April 1944.

# Bibliography

Adam, Karl *Una Sancta in Katholischer Sicht*. Translated Cecily Hastings, Coming Home Resource,2000.

Adenauer, Konrad, *Address to Munich Conference* Bulletin of the Press and Information Office of the Federal Government NO.139 of July 1960.

Asmussen, Hans Legacy https://evangelische-widerstand.de.php?type=document&id =206&1=

Asmussen, Hans, Ed., The Unfinished Reformation Fides, 1961,

Barth, Karl. *Letter endorsing Hans Küng and Justification* https://postbarthian.com/2014/08/04/karl-barths-letter-endorsing-hans-kungs-justification/

Bea, Augustin Cardinal, *The Unity of Christians*, Herder and Herder, 1963.

Bente, Gerhard Friedrich and William Hermann Theodore Dau. *The Book of Concord* Concordia Publishing: https://bookofconcord.org/other-resources/sources-and-context/roman-confutation/Accessed 10/29/24

Burgess, Joseph A, ed, *The Role of the Augsburg Confession: Catholic and Lutheran Views*. Fortress Press, 1980.

Chemnitz, Martin, *Examination of the Council of Trent, Part 1* Translated Fred Kramer Concordia 1971

Concordia Theological Quarterly http://www.ctsfw.net/media/pdfs/klugutherscontribution.pdf

Dawson, Christopher, *The Dividing of Christendom*, Doubleday, 1965.

Eck, Johann 404 Articles, March 1530 : The dedication / translated by J. Bodensieck ; Preface to the printed edition / translated by H.E. Jacobs ; The 404 Articles / translated by H.E. Jacobs in J.M. Reu A Collection of Sources.

Flannery, Austin, O.P. *Vatican II Council: The Conciliar and Post Conciliar Documents*. Dei Verbum, Fowler Wright 1980

Forell, George Wolfgang and James McCue, Eds, *Confessing One Faith: A Joint Commentary on the Augsburg Confession by Lutheran and Catholic Theologians*. Augsburg Publishing House 1980.

Gumbel, Nicky *The Alpha Course* https:en.wikipedia.org/wiki/Alpha_Course

Kolb, Robert, Email Conversation:Rosin, Robert, *Sources and Contexts of the book of Concord* Fortress 2001

Küng, Hans *No peace among the nations*: https://www.goodreads.com/work/quotes/84111

Lackmann, Max, *The Augsburg Confession and Catholic Unity*, Herder and Herder, 1963.
Laros, Matthias, *Una Sancta-Einigung 1 Rundbrief* September 1946
Lehmann, Karl and Wolfhart Pannenberg, *The Condemnations of the Reformation Era: Do they still apply?* Trans. Margaret Kohl, Fortress 1990.
Lortz, Joseph, *The Reformation in Germany Vol.1*. Darton Longman and Todd, 1968.
Luther Martin 95 Theses https://www.luther.de/en/95thesen.html
Luther, Martin The Epistle of St James https: https://zondervnacademic.com/blog/martin-luther-james-bible
Lutheran World Federation: Common Word: Preparing for the 500th anniversary of the Augsburg Confession. Lutheran World assembly. https://2023.lwfassembly.org/common-word-preparing-500th-anniversary-augsburg-confession#: accessed 10/29/24
McCain, Paul T., Ed., *The Augsburg Confession, The Concordia Reader's Edition*. Concordia Publishing, 2005–6
Medick, Hans and Pamela Selwyn, Historical event and Contemporary experience: the capture and destruction of Magdeburg in 1631 History workshop Journal No 52 OUP
Melanchthon, Phillip *The Apology of Melanchthon*. The Lutheran Confessions, Concordia 2005
Meumann, Markus and Niefanger, Dirk *Ein Schauplatz heber Angst:Wahmehung und Darstellung von Gewalt im 17. Jahrhundert* Göttingen:Wallstein 1997
New York Times *Pope Saint John Paul II Praises Luther at 500th anniversary of birth*. https://www.nytimes.com/1983/11/06/world/pope-praises-luther-in-an-appeal-for-unity-on-protest-anniversary.html
Newman, John Henry Cardinal, *Apologia pro vita Sua*. Dover, 2005.
Osborne Fr Kenan, *A History of the Ordained Ministry in the Roman Catholic Church*, Paulist, 1998.
Pfnür, Vinzenz, *Einig in der Rechtfertigungslehre?* Wiesbaden Franz Steiner 1970
Pope Adrian, *Abominations of the Church*: https://www.vatican.va/roman_curia/congregations/cfaith/cti_documents/rc_con_cfaith_doc_20000307_memory-reconc-itc_en.html
Pope Francis *Address to Leaders of Charismatic Renewal*. 2019. https://www.charis.international/en/address-of-his-holiness-pope-francis-to-the-participants-in-the-charis-international-conference-for-the-catholic-charismatic-renewal/
Pope Saint John Paul II *Asks pardon for the Church*. https://www.washingtonpost.com/archive/politics/2000/03/13/pope-asks-pardon-for-sins-of-church/9efdf34b-7912-489f-a6d0-b01eb57c64d6/
Pope Saint John Paul II, *Ut Unum Sint: On Commitment to Ecumenism*. http://www.vatican.va/content/john-paul-ii/en/encyclicals/documents.
Pope Saint John XXIII *Prayer for new Pentecost*. chrome-extension://efaidnbmnnnibpcajpcglclefindmkaj/https://www.pentecosttodayusa.org/wp-content/uploads/2022/02/Burning-Bush-Novena2015.pdf
Ratzinger, Fr Joseph/Pope Benedict XVI Theological Highlights of Vatican II Paulist Press 1966
Ratzinger, Joseph, *The Catechism of the Catholic Church*, USCCB 2000.
Renzikowski, Christoph, *Generalprobe für das zweite vatikanische Konzil*, Domradio. 2010.
Reu, Johann Michael, *The Augsburg Confession: A Collection of Sources*, Wartburg, 1930.

# Bibliography

Schmidt Stjepan, *Augustin Bea*, New City Press 1992

Schroeder, H.J. O.P. The Canons and Decrees of the Council of Trent, Tan Books 19 78.

Steineck, Gundrun, Vorsitzende of the Oekumenische Kreise in Hofheim, Bavaria, Conversation with Author, 2024

Stevenson, Lilian, *Max Josef Metzger Priest and Martyr 1887–1944*.S.P.C.K, 1952.

Swidler, Leonard and Cormac O'Duffy, *The Priest and the Führer*, Ipub Global Connection. 2024.

Swidler, Leonard, *Bloodwitness for Peace and unity The Life of Max Josef Metzger*. Ecumenical Press,1977

Swidler, Leonard, *The Ecumenical Vanguard: The History of the Una Sancta Movement*. Duquesne University Press, 1980

Time Magazine *Article on Jesus Revolution* June 1971

USCCB: Call for Joint Study of Augsburg Confession www.usccb.org/news/2023/vatican-lutheran-officials-call-for-joint-study-augsburg-confession

Vandiver,Elizabeth, Ralph Keen and Thomas D. Frazel, *Luther's Lives: Two contemporary accounts of Martin Luther*, Manchester University Press, 2002.

Varican News: June 25 2021: Pope Francis with Archbishop Panto Filibus Musa President of LWF: https://2023. www.vaticannews.va/en/pope/news/2021-26/pope-francis-world-lutheran-federation-conflict-to-communion.html. Accessed 10/29/24

Thornton, Bro Andrew OSB, Translator. Preface to the Complete Edition of Luther's Latin Works (1545) by Dr. Martin Luther, 1483–1546 from the "Vorrede zu Band I der Opera Latina der Wittenberger Ausgabe. 1545" in vol. 4 of _Luthers Werke in Auswahl_, ed. Otto Clemen, 6th ed., (Berlin: de Gruyter. 1967). pp. 421–28. (c)1983 by Saint Anselm Abbey. Project Wittenburg https://sourcebooks.web.fordham.edu/mod/1519luther-tower.asp

Vatican Documents Pius XII, Mystici Corporis https:// www.vatican.va/content/pius-xii/en/encyclicals/documents/hf_p-xii_enc.29061943-mystici-corporis-christi.html

Vereb, Jerome-Michael, C.P. *"Because he was a German!" Cardinal Bea and the origins of Roman Catholic Engagement in the Ecumenical Movement*. Eerdmans,2006.

Von le Fort, Gertrude, *Magdeburgische Hochzeit*, Insel Verlag, 1938.

Wengert, Timothy J. Essay 4 Phillip Melanchthon's Last Word to Cardinal Lorenzo Campaggio. https://doi.org/10.13109/9783666550478 Accessed 10/29/24

Wikipedia hrrps://en.wikipedia.org/wiki Diogo de Andrara

Wikipedia The Diet of Ravensburg, http://en.wikipedia.org/wiki/Diet of Regensburg: Accessed 10/29/24

Wikipedia: Oecolampadius https;//en.wikipedia.org/wiki/Johannes _Oecolampadius.

Wikipedia: Paiva de Andrade https://en.wikipedia.org/wiki/Diogo_de_Paiva_de_Andrade Accessed 1029/24

Wikipedia: The Leipzig Debate https: en.wikipedia.org/wiki/Leipzig Debate. Accessed 10/29/24

Wikipedia: The Strasbourg Bishops War https://en.wiki/Strasbourg_Bishops%27_War

Wikipedia: World Missionary Conference https://en.wipipedia.org/wiki/1910_World_Missionary_Conference

Wood, Susan K and Timothy J. Wengert. *A Shared Spiritual Journey Lutherans and Catholics Travelling toward Unity*. Paulist,2016.

www.ingramcontent.com/pod-product-compliance
Lightning Source LLC
Chambersburg PA
CBHW051058160426
43193CB00010B/1229